Middle Eastern Minorities

Between Integration and Conflict

Moshe Ma'oz

Policy Papers no. 50

THE WASHINGTON INSTITUTE FOR NEAR EAST POLICY

© 1999 by the Washington Institute for Near East Policy

Published in 1999 in the United States of America by the Washington Institute for Near East Policy, 1828 L Street NW, Suite 1050, Washington, DC 20036.

Library of Congress Cataloging-in-Publication Data

Moshe Ma'oz
   Middle Eastern minorities : between integration and conflict / Moshe Ma'oz.
         p.   cm. — (Policy papers ; no. 50)
      Includes bibliographical references
      ISBN 0-944029-33-7 (pbk.)
      1. Religious minorities—Middle East—History—19th century. 2. Religious minorities—Middle East—History—20th century. 3. Minorities—Middle East. 4. Religion and politics—Middle East. 5. Religion and culture—Middle East.   I. Title. II. Policy papers (Washington Institute for Near East Policy) ; no. 50.
   BL1600.M36 1999
   305.6'0956—dc21   99-048682
                                                             CIP

Cover photos © Corbis.
Cover design by Monica Neal Hertzman.

The Author

M oshe Ma'oz is professor of Islamic and Middle Eastern studies at the Hebrew University of Jerusalem and,
formerly, the director of the university's Harry S Truman Research Institute for the Advancement of Peace. He received
his doctoral degree, on the modern history of the Middle
East, from Oxford University, and has published several books
and articles on Syrian and Palestinian history and politics and
Arab–Israeli relations. His most recent book is *Syria and Israel: From War to Peacemaking* (Oxford, 1995).

Dr. Ma'oz was a visiting research fellow at The Washington Institute in 1997, when he began work on this project.

• • •

Table of Contents

Acknowledgments

I wish to thank The Washington Institute's executive director, Robert Satloff, and the staff of the Institute for their hospitality, which enabled me to prepare this paper. As this paper is a part of a larger research project on Middle Eastern minorities, I would also like to thank the Leonard Davis Institute and the Harry S Truman Institute for their support, and my research assistant, Yusri Khizran, for his help.

Moshe Ma'oz
Jerusalem
September 1999

Preface

For the past half-century, governments, diplomats, journalists and scholars have tended to view the Middle East through the lens of the Arab–Israeli conflict. Solve that dispute, many argued, and the region would be transformed into a more normal collection of nation-states, without the omnipresent threat of instability, insecurity, and war.

In reality, however, the Arab–Israeli dispute is only one of the many ethnic and religious conflicts that color Middle East politics. And the achievement of "comprehensive Arab-Israeli peace" will not itself usher in a period intercommunal and interreligious harmony. On the contrary, it is only more likely to expose the fault lines within societies and between countries that many rulers across the region have masked for decades behind the façade of "the struggle for Palestine."

Beneath the surface in most Middle Eastern countries are simmering ethnic and religious conflicts that lack only a lighted fuse to explode. Some of these conflicts are well known to Americans, like the communal struggle among Sunni Kurds, Sunni Arabs, and Shi'i Arabs for dominance in Iraq and the Sunni, Christian, Shi'i Muslim, and Druze "warlordism" to which Lebanon descended at the worst of its civil war. Other minority–majority conficts are less well-known but no less volatile: Sunni–'Alawi tensions in Syria, Sunni–Christian/Animist fighting in Sudan, and to a lesser but still potent extent, Sunni–Christian hostility in Egypt.

Not all news is bad, though. In Jordan, for example, the Sunni Arab majority has a long history of positive relations with its Christian and Circassian minority. And as other governments from North Africa to Israel begin to see their minority populations as less threatening, inclusiveness—or at least coexistence—seems more attainable.

In this, The Washington Institute's fiftieth Policy Paper, noted historian Moshe Ma'oz presents a concise survey of majority–minority relations across the Middle East and of the potential for conflict arising from ethnic and religious tensions. Professor Ma'oz brings to this study a detailed knowledge of the politics, society, and culture across this divided region, as well as the sensitivity of a scholar who has studied the communal relations of Middle Eastern peoples from the Ottoman empire through the present day. The Washington Institute is proud to present his cogent analysis as the starting point for policymakers committed to resolving the region's many conflicts.

Mike Stein   Barbi Weinberg
President   Chairman

Executive Summary

Religious and ethnic minorities have significantly influenced political, economic, cultural, and ideological developments in the Middle East for the last two centuries. This study focuses on Egypt, Sudan, and the countries of the Fertile Crescent, some of which have minority populations of 35 percent or more. The relationships of these minorities with the majority population in their respective countries, as well as their interrelations within and across borders, have undergone crucial changes over the generations. In some cases, sections of various religious communities and of small ethnic communities have been gradually integrating into or adjusting to their developing national societies. In others, certain ethnic/nationalist and religious/sectarian conflicts have been aggravated to the point of violence, and, at times, war. This study distinguishes the factors, forces, and circumstances that have affected intercommunal relations in the region—toward both coexistence and antagonism—by examining case studies from the region.

Historical Background

In the Middle East, most non-Sunni and ethnic-minority communities have deep historical roots. Ancient ethnoreligious communities include Copts in Egypt, Assyrians and Kurds in Mesopotamia, Jews in historic Palestine, Shi'is in Iraq and Lebanon, Druze in Lebanon, 'Alawis in Syria, and various Christian sects in most parts of the region. Other communities or minorities arose over the centuries through migration, either from one area of the region to another or from more remote places. During Ottoman rule in the Middle East, the legal, political, and social status of the various minorities were generally determined by religious affiliation rather than by ethnic belonging.

During the nineteenth century, crucial changes occurred in the positions of, and relations between, major religious communities. These changes were influenced partly by Ottoman reforms intended to better the administration, economy, and society in the empire and partly by European ideas and actions. They were accompanied by great violence and contributed to the emergence of new national movements, particularly in the regions of Syria and Lebanon.

Jordan

The Hashemite Kingdom has, to date, been the exemplary Middle Eastern case of peaceful integration of religious and ethnic minorities into their nation-state. This applies to the relatively small communities of Christian Arabs and non-Arab Circassians. This is likely to continue as long as the monarchy maintains its strong control, its constitutional basis, and its process of democratization.

Egypt

Copts have ancient Egyptian origins, share a common social and cultural background with the Muslim majority, constitute a small percentage of the population, and are involved only to a minor extent with foreign powers. Thus, as Egypt's largest minority, Orthodox Copts could have expected the same process of peaceful integration in their national community as Christians experienced in Jordan. In fact a process of integration did begin in the mid-nineteenth century, but it was periodically interrupted by militant Muslim action that caused Muslim–Christian tension and Coptic anxiety. Swings of integration and rejection continued throughout the twentieth century; segregation was the norm under the more authoritarian regimes. Since the mid-1990s, Egyptian security forces have curbed much of the anti-Christian violence. Yet, Copts have continued to suffer from discrimination in certain state institutions, in the public sector, in education, and in the economic field. As they have again become marginalized, they have continued to emigrate.

Egyptian president Hosni Mubarak may be concerned

about the plight of the Copts, but as long as the domestic, liberal, secular, and democratic groups remain small and uninfluential, Mubarak will be unable to ensure the Copts are full and equal members of Egypt's national and political communities. Effective American intervention on behalf of the Copts is not likely to occur, because Egypt is strategically important to the United States.

Arabs and Jews in Pre-1948 Palestine

Christian–Muslim relations in historic Palestine date back to the seventh century Islamic conquest. Christians living in Palestine at that time were arabized. By the twentieth century, a number of Christian Arab intellectuals strove to create a common nonsectarian basis with their Muslim Arab compatriots. They did so by working to revive the Arabic language and culture; introducing fresh patriotic and nationalist ideas; and stressing the potential common threat posed by Jewish Zionist immigrants, who had started to arrive in the early 1880s. In fact, Christian Arabs became leading figures in the pan-Arab, and later Palestinian Arab, nationalist movement. The perceived challenge of the Jewish Zionist minority continued to be a major incentive for Muslim–Christian solidarity, particularly among the elites in the Palestinian national community.

Although Palestinian Arabs were the majority of the population and enjoyed the backing of Arab neighbors, the Jewish immigrants were able to create a powerful national community during the British Mandatory period. The success of the Jewish Zionist minority in achieving statehood in May 1948 dealt a serious blow to pan-Arab ideology. Sunni Arab leaders were especially worried that the Jewish minority's success would act as a precedent for other minorities in the region, encouraging them to follow suit and dismember their respective countries.

Arabs in Israel

During its first two decades of statehood, Israel treated its Arab minority as a potentially subversive "fifth column" and imposed strict restrictions on Israeli Arabs. As Israel grew stronger and began to feel more confident, it granted more equal rights to its Arab citizens. Nevertheless, it continues to view the Arabs not as a national minority but as separate religious communities that should adjust to or integrate into the Jewish state. Here, the community that has most thoroughly adjusted has been the Druze.

Over time, Israel's Arabs moved from alienation to accommodation; they did not revolt against their government, and only a minuscule number have been involved in acts of sabotage or espionage. Yet, many are unable to identify with a Jewish Zionist state. Most have identified on many levels with Palestinians in the West Bank and Gaza Strip, particularly since 1967. After the signing of the Oslo Declaration of Principles in 1993, Israeli Arabs hoped that the final settlement between Israel and the Palestine Liberation Organization (PLO) would solve the conflict between their people and their state.

Any future Palestinian state would have its own minority: Palestinian Christians. Emigration has reduced their numbers to about 4 percent of the Palestinian population today. Nevertheless, the longtime association of Muslims and Christians working together for Palestinian nationhood is likely to continue, especially among politicians, intellectuals, professionals, and the new middle classes.

Lebanon

For several decades after 1943, Lebanon's Maronite Christian, Shi'i Muslim, and Sunni elites cooperated in a pluralist, quasi-democratic Lebanese regime in which the Maronites were dominant. But a shift in the demographic balance in favor of the Muslim communities, Arab nationalist radicalization, the military Palestinian presence, and Syrian and Israeli interventions all relegated the Maronites to a defensive, militant position. Following the bloody and largely communal-religious civil war of 1975–1990, the Muslim communities received a larger share of power in government institutions, under Syrian dictation. This new balance will likely persist for some time—provided Syrian hegemony continues.

In some respects, the Lebanese system has reverted to

the pre–civil war era. On the one hand, sectarian tendencies have remained high, but on the other, alliances of Shi'is, Sunnis, Druze, and Christians have emerged in the parliament. With its ultimate goal of turning Lebanon into an Islamic state, however, Hizballah may in the future pose a fundamental challenge to the Lebanese political system.

Syria

Attempts at creating a nonsectarian national community in Syria took place as early as century before the ascendancy of the Ba'th regime, particularly during the regime of the semi-independent Syrian Arab state, in 1918–1920. The subsequent French mandate, however, promoted religious sectarian separatism. Only after the French had gone, in 1946, were Syrian leaders in a position to attempt national integration. The accelerated pace of modernization and the creation of a national school system contributed to drawing the minorities and other sections of the population closer to each other.

Yet, many Sunni Muslims considered the Ba'thist–'Alawi regimes in power since the 1960s not only illegitimate and oppressive but also heretical and anti-Islamic. Since the late 1980s, Syrian president Hafiz al-Asad has expanded his efforts to gain allegiance, or at least to secure the acquiescence, of Sunni Muslims. He has promoted among Syrian Arabs a national integration whose main components have been the ideas of Arab nationalism, Syrian patriotism, and nonsectarian unity.

As for non-Arab ethnic minorities, most have been at least partly arabized and have integrated into, or adjusted to, the Syrian state. Although the urban Kurds in particular have largely assimilated, many among the tribal and rural Kurds in the Jazira region and north of Aleppo have, since the 1950s, been periodically subjected to harsh measures aimed at suppressing their ethnic identity.

Iraq

The Ba'th Sunni minority regime in Iraq rules over a Shi'i community that constitutes more than 50 percent of the population and a sizable Kurdish population of about 20 percent.

Given the topography of the Kurdish region in Iraq, the persistence of Kurdish nationalism and of Shi'i radicalism, and the periodic involvement of external powers, Iraq has encountered perhaps the hardest obstacles in its attempts to create a national community. In the late 1970s and in 1991, militant Shi'is rebelled against the government. Saddam Husayn's regime brutally crushed these uprisings, such that today many Iraqi Shi'is opt instead for full integration and participation in the political and socioeconomic systems, compatible with their demographic strength.

While seldom demanding full independence, Kurdish nationalists have regularly demanded political–territorial or administrative autonomy in their region, proper representation in state institutions, and a share of the oil revenues in Kurdistan. Most Iraqi governments rejected the Kurds' demands for territorial autonomy and refused to grant the Kurds a proportional share of governmental power and of state resources. Some regimes would promise to meet Kurdish demands but would then avoid implementing their pledges fully, while fostering internal Kurdish disputes and thereby attempting to advance their own control over Kurdish areas.

The future status of Iraqi Kurdistan depends largely on the positions and policies of outside powers. Although the United States may again protect this region from Iraqi threats, it remains unwilling to commit its policies, resources, and troops to the creation of a viable Kurdish autonomy, let alone independence. Turkey and Iran are also opposed to an independent Kurdish entity, because it might set a precedent for their own Kurdish populations. Moreover, Saddam's Iraq vehemently opposes Kurdish separatism and would sooner make concessions to its Shi'i population, thereby playing the Shi'is against the Kurds.

Southern Sudan

The problem of southern Sudan seems unresolvable in the near future. The southern Sudanese constitute approximately 30 percent of the country's population, are largely animist or Christian, are divided among several ethnic African groups and many tribes, and speak dozens of dialects (English is their common language). Successive Sudanese governments, even before the country's independence, have treated southerners with contempt, animosity, and brutality, and regarded them as pagan, primitive, and fragmented.

Southern Sudan borders on non-Arab African countries whose populations are related to some southern Sudanese tribes, share ethnic African solidarity with them, or both. These populations and their governments, however, do not want to compound their own economic and social difficulties by uniting with southern Sudan. They have instead sought a political solution to the problem to preserve the African ethnic cultural character of the South and prevent its forced assimilation—namely Arabization and Islamization—by Sudanese governments based in the North. Although some Sudanese governments have at times agreed to such a solution, they have not fully implemented their promises or bilateral accords, and successive regimes have attempted to Arabize and Islamize the South. Thus the conflict has continued.

For various reasons—including a desire to avoid a precedent of secession on the continent and avoiding the burden of southern refugees—few East African states, and indeed few southern Sudanese, have advocated the creation of an independent state.

Conclusion

Non-Sunni Arab communities in the region have experienced unequal changes—sometimes even upheavals—in their political status and in their relations with the ruling elites. Generally speaking, Christians in the upper and middle classes have integrated themselves into the more secular societies— Jordan, Syria, Iraq, the Palestinian community, and, periodically, Egypt. In countries with militant Islamic movements or policies, however, Christians have been treated with suspicion, hatred, and occasional violence. Most religious minorities in other Arab countries will probably continue to integrate into, or adjust to, their respective nation-states at different degrees and pace. The more secular, liberal, or democratic these states become, the greater the pace and degree of integration would be advanced.

Ethnic minorities have generally not assimilated as well. The large populations of ethnic minorities in southern Sudan and Iraqi Kurdistan are doomed to carry on their struggle for self-determination or self-government until a truly democratic system replaces the authoritarian, repressive governments in their countries, or until a powerful international intervention occurs on their behalf.

Israel, of course, has its own ethnic minority problem. It wants to coexist peacefully with its Arab community while preserving its Jewish democratic character. Despite its initial false start and continuing problems, Israel has made a strong effort to integrate its Arab minority. Further improving this process and preventing a possible serious crisis with its ethnic–national Arab minority are additional rationales behind Israel's efforts to seek a negotiated settlement with the PLO.

Irrespective of the state of Israeli–Arab relations, major ethnic conflicts in the Middle East remain unresolved and dangerous. Washington can help the Iraqi Kurds and southern Sudanese to forge their de facto self-rule. At the same time, Washington could encourage and support the formation of intercommunal coalitions that strive to replace repressive regimes and establish federal democratic systems. It can also encourage other countries to continue their positive treatment of minorities by making such treatment a condition for U.S. financial assistance. In general, however, the United States is unlikely to intervene vigorously on behalf of oppressed ethnic minorities and religious communities. Rather, chances are high that it will try to avoid alienating its Arab allies and other Arab states while advancing its strategic aims in the Middle East—namely, preventing regional conflicts, resolving the Arab–Israeli dispute, and establishing a regional security system under its auspices.

Chapter 1

Introduction

Religious and ethnic minorities have significantly influenced political, economic, cultural, and ideological developments in the Middle East for the last two centuries. On the average, the Middle Eastern countries on which this study focuses—the Fertile Crescent, Egypt, and Sudan—have minority populations of about 35 percent, though in the larger region of the Middle East and North Africa minorities constitute on average only about 20 percent of the population.[1] Their mutual relations with the majority populations in their respective countries, as well as their interrelations, have undergone crucial changes over the generations, variously characterized by trends of accommodation and adjustment or conflict and segregation.

These changing relations have been particularly conspicuous during the last several decades in the newly emerging nation-states in the Middle East. Thus, on the one hand, sections of various religious communities and of small ethnic communities have been gradually integrating into or adjusting to the developing national societies in Egypt, Jordan, Syria, and Iraq, whereas in Lebanon a unique intercommunal coexistence and cooperation was established and endured until 1975. On the other hand, ethnic/nationalist and religious/sectarian conflicts were aggravated to the point of violence, and in some cases war, in Iraq, Sudan, Lebanon, and Syria, claiming six times more lives (1.2 million total) than all the Arab–Israeli wars combined (200,000 total). These internal conflicts represent the "greatest threat to the security of the states in the region" in the 1990s, to quote the Egyptian scholar Saad Eddin Ibrahim.[2]

In outlining the major changes in the sociopolitical posi-

1

tion of the various religious and ethnic minorities since the nineteenth century, this study will attempt to distinguish the factors, forces, and circumstances that have affected inter-communal relations in the region, toward both coexistence and antagonism. I shall particularly dwell upon the protracted ethnic conflicts in Iraq and Sudan, as well as on the upheav-als in intersectarian relations in Lebanon, Iraq, and Syria during the last several decades. Finally, I shall try evaluate the effect of these developments on the cohesion of the relevant nation-states and on regional security, as well as on Arab–Israeli relations and on U.S. policy.

Definitions

Before commencing this review, we should define the terms "religious minorities" and "ethnic minorities" as they apply in the Middle East. The simplest definition, initially suggested by Albert Hourani,[3] depicts the minorities as those commu-nities that differ from the Sunni Arab majority in their religious affiliation and/or their ethnocultural identity. These can be subdivided into the following categories:

- **Religious communities** that are non-Sunni Muslim, but that are ethnically or culturally Arab, namely most Chris-tian communities—Greek Orthodox, Greek Catholic, Copts, Maronites, Latins, and Protestants; and the vari-ous Muslim heterodox sects, notably Shi'is, 'Alawis, Druze, and Isma'ilis.
- **Ethnic or national groups** that are either non-Arab but Sunni Muslim, such as the Kurds, Turkomans, and Circassians; or neither Arab nor Muslim—Jews, Arme-nians, Assyrians, and southern Sudanese tribes.

These distinctions between the majority populations and the various minorities apply to the Middle East region as a whole, and to most of its states, with the exception of the following:

- **Iraq**, whose majority population (some 60 percent) has been for generations Shi'i Arab, but whose Sunni Arab ruling group (some 20 percent) has had a superior po-litical position and socioeconomic conditions than the majority Shi'i population.

- **Lebanon**, which consists of several religious communities—Christian and Muslim—with no one forming a clear majority.
- **Palestine/Israel**, where the Sunni Arab majority population in British Mandatory Palestine was transformed in 1948 into an ethnic minority in the predominantly Jewish State of Israel. (For reasons of historic and geographic simplicity, when discussing the origins of peoples, this book will refer to the region that fell under the British Mandate as Palestine.)

Notes

1. See Saad Eddin Ibrahim, *Management of Ethnic Issues in the Arab World,* Strategic papers no. 26 (Cairo: Al-Ahram Center for Political and Strategic Studies, February 1995), p. 5. For more data and a breakdown of the minority population into demographic proportions, see tables in the appendix.

2. Ibid., p. 3.

3. Albert H. Hourani, *Minorities in the Arab World* (London: Oxford University Press, 1947); see also Ibrahim, *Management,* pp. 4, 22–24.

Chapter 2

Historical Background

M ost religious- and ethnic-minority communities in the Middle East originate either from the region's ancient pre-Arab inhabitants or from the three monotheistic religions and their subsequent offshoots; some originate from both cultural and religious antiquity. Examples of these ancient ethnoreligious minorities include Copts in Egypt, Assyrians and Kurds in Mesopotamia, Jews in Palestine (later exiled to other parts of the region), Shi'is in Iraq and Lebanon, Druze in Lebanon, 'Alawis in Syria, and various Christian sects in most parts of the region. Other communities or minorities arose over the centuries through migration within the region from one area to another or through migration from more remote places: Turkomans came from Anatolia to Syria and Iraq, Kurds from Kurdistan to Syria, North African Arabs from the Maghreb to Syria and Palestine, Druze from Lebanon to Syria and Palestine, Circassians and Chechens from the Caucasus to Syria and Transjordan, Armenians from Turkey to Lebanon, and Jews from Spain and Central and Eastern Europe to Syria and Palestine.

During the many centuries of Ottoman rule in the Middle East, the legal, political, and social status of the various minorities were generally determined by religious affiliation rather than by ethnic belonging. Thus, all Sunni Muslim communities, regardless of their ethnic origin—Arab, Turk, Kurd, or Circassian—were considered full members of the Islamic *'umma* (community) and formed the ruling elites. For example, Salah al-Din, or Saladin, the great twelfth-century Muslim ruler, was a Kurd.

In contrast, non-Sunnis were regarded as inferior subjects (Christians and Jews) or as illegitimate denominations (the heterodox sects) and thus were officially discriminated against or persecuted by the state; they were also occasionally mistreated by conservative or fanatic Sunni Muslims.

Muslims, Christians, and Jews

Christians and Jews, the *Ahl al-Kitab* (people of the Book, belonging to the monotheist beliefs), experienced dual-level treatment in Ottoman Muslim state and society.[1] On the one hand, they were granted *dhimma* (state protection) and certain autonomous privileges in matters of religious worship and were allowed to exercise their own judgment in matters such as personal status and education. Jewish and Christian individuals periodically held senior positions in the courts of sultans and provincial rulers, as financial advisers, physicians, translators, and the like. Others were even occasionally admitted to and fairly treated in Islamic law (*shari'a*) courts.[2]

On the other hand, Christians and Jews were essentially considered and treated as inferior subjects in state institutions and by many Muslims. They paid a *jizya* (special poll tax) and could hold only subordinate positions in the service of Muslims, but never senior political posts, unless they converted to Islam. Periodically, they were also subjected to various restrictions, such as those concerning worship and attire, and were molested by Muslim officials and fanatics.

Changes in the Nineteenth Century

On the state level, Christians and Jews were officially and gradually granted equal legal and political status under the Ottoman *Tanzimat* reforms—aimed at reorganizing and improving the administration, economy, and society in the empire—of 1839, 1856, and the 1876 constitution.[3] Yet, these reforms were only partly implemented, sometimes under European inducement or pressure, owing to strong objection by conservative Ottoman officials, Muslim religious leaders (the *'ulama*), and other traditional groups. Indeed, many Muslims were concerned lest the equal status granted to Christians radically change the character of the Islamic state, put it under Christian–European rule, or in any way undermine their own political, social, and economic interests.

In several places, the Christians themselves partly contributed to these Muslim concerns by seeking European protection and intervention, insisting on invoking their equal rights without delay and undertaking public actions that provoked Muslim antagonism. The traditional Muslim feeling of contempt toward Christians consequently turned into resentment, fear, and hostility and resulted in several anti-Christian and anti-European riots in some parts of the empire. In Damascus, for example, Muslims (and some Druze) massacred thousands of Christians—men, women and children—in 1860, looting and destroying their churches.[4]

In contrast, Christians in Egypt, notably the Arabized Copts, generally continued to coexist tolerably or even peacefully with their Muslim neighbors under the reforms of Muhammad 'Ali and his successors, who granted them equal status in the state. This result was achieved because of strict government control, the traditional affinity between Muslims and Copts, and the absence of special links between Copts and the European powers.

Like the Copts in Egypt, Jews in the Ottoman Empire were not harmed by Muslims during the reform era, as they continued to behave like small, humble, and apolitical communities,[5] stressing their unconditional loyalty to the state and refraining from demonstrating their new liberties, particularly in times of crisis. In many places Jews continued to enjoy more preferential treatment from Muslim authorities and by their neighbors than did Christians. For example, during the 1860 massacre in Damascus, Jews were not affected at all. In fact, they even sympathized with the Muslim rioters, largely in revenge for the anti-Jewish blood libel propagated by Damascene Christians in 1840.

Christians of various denominations and in various places in the Ottoman Empire and Egypt would periodically accuse Jews of killing Christians, usually children, and using their blood for baking Passover *matzot*. These attempts to dehumanize and destroy Jews reflected the prolonged religious antagonism between Christians and Jews. This antagonism first manifested itself in the region as blood libels, in part because of the growing Christian–European influence of the nineteenth century. Such accusations were sometimes exploited by Christians in the fierce competition with Jews over positions in the Ottoman financial administration as well as in trade, commerce, and banking.[6]

To be sure, intersectarian competition and strife was not confined to Christians and Jews or Muslims and Christians. It also characterized the interrelations between most other communities and sects in various parts of the region. As a British resident of Damascus observed in the early 1870s, perhaps with some exaggeration: "They hate one another. The Sunnites excommunicate the Shiahs, and both hate the Druze, and detest the Ansariyyahs ['Alawis]; the Maronites do not love anybody but themselves and are duly abhorred by all, the Greek Orthodox abominate the Greek Catholics and the Latins; all despise the Jews."[7]

As regards the heterodox sects—Shi'is, 'Alawis, Druze, and Ismai'ilis—the Sunni Muslim state and religious leaders considered them deviators from Islam. In some cases, particularly as regards the 'Alawis, these sects were considered heretics. Accordingly, the Ottoman government persecuted them periodically, in addition to its attempts to levy taxes on these unruly groups and conscript their youngsters.[8] To avoid persecution, some small heterodox communities occasionally posed as Sunnis, in accordance with their *taqiyya* (caution, discreetness) rule. But the large heterodox centers remained secluded and fortified, and certain groups among them engaged periodically in armed conflict with Sunnis and Christians over economic resources and political control, among other issues.

For example, in Mount Lebanon, Druze–Maronite relations, which for generations had been collaborative, changed significantly in the late eighteenth century because of the political ascendancy, economic prosperity, and cultural revival of the Maronites—with French help—which seriously threatened the traditional Druze hegemony in the Mount. Consequently, a Druze–Maronite civil war erupted in the 1840s, culminating in 1860 with a victory for the Druze and many lives lost for the Maronite Christians.[9]

In sum, alongside the evolution in the traditional pattern of intercommunal coexistence, there occurred during the nineteenth century crucial changes in the positions of, and relations between, major religious communities. Influenced partly by the Tanzimat reforms and partly by European ideas and actions, these changes were accompanied for the first time by great violence and contributed to the emergence of new national movements, particularly in the regions of Syria and Lebanon.

Notes

1. On the status of *Ahl al-Kitab* under Islam see, for example, Gustave E. Von Grunebaum, *Medieval Islam* (Chicago: University of Chicago Press, 1953), chapter 6.

2. See, for instance, Amnon Cohen and Elisheva Simon-Pikali, *Jews in the Muslim Religious Court* (Jerusalem: Yad Yitzhak Ben-Zvi, 1993; in Hebrew).

3. See Roderic H. Davison, *Reform in the Ottoman Empire, 1856–1876* (Princeton: Princeton University Press, 1963).

4. See Moshe Ma'oz, *Ottoman Reform in Syria and Palestine, 1840–1861: The Impact of the Tanzimat on Politics and Society* (Oxford: Clarendon Press, 1968), pp. 200–238; idem, "Communal Conflicts in Ottoman Syria," in Benjamin Braude and Bernard Lewis, eds., *Christians and Jews in the Ottoman Empire: The Functioning of a Plural Society* (New York: Holmes and Meier, 1982), vol. II, pp. 91–105.

5. See Abdolonyme Ubicini, *Letters on Turkey* (London: John Murray, 1856), vol. II, p. 347.

6. See Avigdor Levy, ed., *The Jews of the Ottoman Empire* (Princeton, N.J.: Darwin Press, 1994), p. 541.

7. Isabel Burton, *The Inner Life in Syria* (London, 1875), pp. 105–106.

8. See, for example, Ma'oz, *Ottoman Reform*, pp. 108–111; also relevant is Martin Kramer, ed., *Shi'ism, Resistance, and Revolution* (Boulder, Colo.: Westview, 1987), particularly his chapter, "Syria's Alawis and Shi'ism," pp. 238–239.

9. See Antun Dahir al-Aqiqi (Malcolm H. Kerr, trans.), *Lebanon in the Last Years of Feudalism, 1840–1868* (Beirut: American University of Beirut, 1959).

Chapter 3

Minorities, Nationalism, and Nation-States: An Overview

The events of 1860 in Lebanon and Damascus marked a turning point for Christians in the Levant. Many of them— hundreds of thousands—emigrated, despairing of peaceful coexistence with Muslims. Many others who stayed further consolidated their communal cohesion and seclusion, with European backing. The Maronites in of Mount Lebanon, in particular, utilized the special autonomous status imposed in 1861 by the European powers to cultivate their newly emerged national community and build a political, economic, and cultural infrastructure for a future Christian Lebanese nation-state.

But after the creation of Greater Lebanon (1920), and because of various demographic, economic, and political calculations, most Maronites chose to settle peacefully for a unique type of Lebanese Arab state, alongside their neighboring communities—Sunni, Shi'i, Druze, Greek Orthodox, Greek Catholic, and Armenian. Unfortunately, this singular multicommunal system collapsed in 1975 in a violent civil war. Since the early 1990s, the previous system has been reinstated, albeit with certain changes and under Syrian control.

In Egypt, the Copts, who enjoyed equal rights and duties since the mid-nineteenth century, were largely integrated into the Egyptian national movement alongside Syrian Christians, Armenians, and some Jews. In 1882, these groups jointly struggled against the British occupation. Considering themselves as "the true Egyptians," Copts preferred the liberal wing of the movement, the National Party, whose leader, Mustafa Kamil, declared that "Copts and Muslims are one people,

11

linked in nationality, traditions, character, and mentality, . . . we as Egyptians, Copts and Muslims, we talk about religion only in the church or mosque."[1]

Yet the Copts were deeply concerned about the pan-Islamic and anti-Christian tendencies that developed in the National Party, particularly after the death of Mustafa Kamil in 1908 and the assassination in 1910 of the Coptic prime minister, Boutros Ghali, by a young nationalist. But Coptic–Muslim dissension, publicly manifested in 1911 by the assembling of two rival congresses, was healed to a large extent during the 1919 revolution against the British protectorate ("The unity of the Crescent and the Cross") and under the leadership of Sa'd Zaghlul. His first independent cabinet, in 1922, included one Jewish and two Coptic ministers; a Copt also served as head of the Chamber of Deputies. Yet, since the 1940s, Muslim–Coptic relations have gradually deteriorated and Copts have become marginalized in the Egyptian polity and economy.

In other parts of the region, notably in Syria, a small number of Christian intellectuals sought to create a new nonsectarian basis for coexistence with their Muslim fellow countrymen, namely, a common patriotic attachment to the homeland, interwoven with a generic Arab cultural and linguistic heritage. Yet, these European-inspired notions of patriotism and subsequently of nationalism were still alien to or premature among other Arabic-speaking religious communities—Sunni, Shi'i, 'Alawi, and Druze—as well as among many Arabic-speaking Christians themselves. Only in the later years of the Ottoman Empire, in reaction to the tyrannical rule of Sultan Abdul Hamid II (1876–1908) and the anti-Arab policies of the Young Turks (1908–1914), did Muslim Arab intellectuals develop nationalist awareness. This awareness initially developed separately from that espouse by Christian Arabs. During the period of the French Mandate (1920-1946), however, the Sunni-led national and party politics of Syria, as well as the country's military, gradually integrated Christians, followed by 'Alawis and Druze. In 1966, members of Syria's 'Alawi minority—which constitutes 12 percent of the population—seized and retained the reins of power, despite serious Sunni-Muslim resistance.

The late-nineteenth-century emergence of the Jewish Zionist national movement in Europe, followed by the increasing immigration of these Zionist Jews to Palestine, facilitated the efforts of Christian Arab intellectuals to enlist the cooperation of their Muslim compatriots in a common struggle against the Zionist challenge. This struggle arose first under the banner of Arab nationalism and subsequently of Palestinian Arab nationalism. Nevertheless, the small Jewish Zionist community in Palestine—some 60,000 in 1917, compared to 600,000 Arabs—prevailed against the Palestinian Arabs to became the only ethnic-national minority in the Middle East to succeed in realizing its national aspirations, with the establishment of the State of Israel in 1948. Since then, the Jewish state has faced the political challenge of its Arab Palestinian minority and, since 1967, the national aspirations of the Palestinian Arabs in the West Bank and the Gaza Strip.

In Iraq, the Arab nationalist movement emerged later than in other parts of the region, both because of the country's limited exposure to European ideas and because of its small Christian Arab communities. Initially starting as a reaction to Young Turk policies, an Iraqi Arab nationalism developed under the British occupation (starting in 1914) and Mandate (1920–1932); its first manifestation was the 1920 revolt against the British. Uniquely, here Sunni Arab nationalists cooperated with Shi'i religious leaders and tribal chiefs in a short rebellion against the European Christian foreign occupier. Subsequently, Shi'is—and for a while also Jews—participated in the Sunni-led Iraqi Arab national community. Yet, many Shi'is in the South remained underprivileged and developed a religiously inspired opposition to the Sunni Arab minority rule. In the northern parts of Iraq, two non-Arab ethnic minorities developed national aspirations: the Christian Assyrians (or Nestorians), who had been dislocated from eastern Turkey and settled by the British in 1918 around Zakhu and Dahuk, and the Sunni Muslim Kurds, to whom the 1920

Treaty of Sévrès had promised a Kurdish autonomy-cum-state, and to whom the British subsequently promised an autonomous region around Mosul.[2] Both of these minorities had distinct encounters with the Sunni state and experienced different consequences. The tiny Assyrian minority (some 20,000) was destroyed and dispersed after the 1933 massacre by Iraqi troops. The large Kurdish community, at 18 percent of the population, gradually transformed from a Muslim religious and tribal society into a national movement that has struggled since the 1920s for political autonomy in Iraqi Kurdistan, though with little success.

On the opposite pole of the Arab world, in southern Sudan, non-Arab African tribes—Christian and pagans—have fought since 1956 for self-determination vis-à-vis the Sunni Arab north, but with no conclusive results. Along with Kurdish northern Iraq, southern Sudan has been the scene of the most violent and acute internal conflict between ethnic minorities and national Arab governments in the region. These conflicts not only threaten the territorial integrity of Iraq and Sudan, but also carry with them serious regional, international, strategic, and security repercussions.

Are these conflicts heading for disaster or settlement? In the case of Iraq, how will the Kurdish–Arab conflict affect the problem of the national integration of the majority Shi'i community with the minority Sunni Arab ruling group? This problem can be compared to the attempts of the 'Alawi minority ruling elite to integrate the majority Sunni into a Syrian national community. What are the prospects in these two cases? No less interesting are the endeavors to rebuild a nation state in multicommunal Lebanon, where the largest group—the Shi'i community—holds only a minor share in political and socioeconomic power. Is Lebanon heading for a new accommodation or a revived conflict among its religious communities?

In all other cases, it would appear that the religious and ethnic minorities have more or less integrated in, accommodated, or adjusted to their nation states, or that they do not pose a serious threat. Thus, these minorities are not exposed to physical elimination or to coercive assimilation. At the top of the "integration scale" are Christian Arabs and Circassians in Jordan and in Syria. Lagging behind are Christians in the Palestinian community and Arabs in Israel; Copts in Egypt and Kurds in Syria are at the bottom of the scale. What, then, are the historical, political, or demographic changes or circumstances underlying these cases and what developments can be expected in each case? The answers to these questions shall constitute the body of chapters 4–11.

Notes

1. Quoted in Doris Behrens-Abouseif, "The Political Situation of the Copts, 1798–1923," in Benjamin Braude and Bernard Lewis, eds., *Christians and Jews in the Ottoman Empire: The Functioning of a Plural Society* (New York: Holmes and Meier, 1982), vol. II, p. 195.

2. See Phebe Marr, *The Modern History of Iraq* (Boulder, Colo.: Westview, 1985), pp. 40–43.

Chapter 4

Integrated Minorities:
The Case of Jordan

J ordan has so far been the exemplary Middle Eastern case
of peaceful integration of religious and ethnic minorities
into their nation-state. This applies to the relatively small communities of Christian Arabs and of non-Arab Circassians, who
have shared common social and cultural habits with their
Muslim Arab compatriots under a strong and fairly liberal
monarchy. (The Jordanians of Palestinian origin will not be
discussed in this essay as a minority case, not only because
numerically they constitute the majority population, but because they share with the veteran Jordanians the same
linguistic and cultural heritage and the Sunni Muslim faith.)

The Emirate of Transjordan, created in 1922, was inhabited in the 1920s by some 250,000 people. The population
rose to slightly less than half a million by 1948, two years before it became the Hashemite Kingdom of Jordan, which then
included the annexed Palestinian West Bank. By 1995, the
population of the East Bank had reached more than four
million. Large sections of the population were initially, and
many still are, nomadic and rural—including the Christian
Arabs and Circassian Muslims. Mostly descendants of the ancient pre-Islamic inhabitants, the Christians—some 30,000 in
the 1920s—belong to the Greek Orthodox, Greek Catholic,
Latin, and Protestant churches. Their percentage of the population has been declining gradually. In 1961 they constituted
6.4 percent of the population, whereas in 1998 they totaled
only 4 percent out of a total Jordanian population of some
4.4 million. (See appendix.)

The Sunni Muslim Circassians—some 12,000 in the 1920s

and 25,000 in 1991—settled in Transjordan after the late 1870s, when they were expelled from the Caucasus by Czarist Russia; they were joined by a small group of mostly Shi'i Muslim Chechens, or Shishanis, who numbered some 2,000 in 1991.[1]

"Rapacious, cruel, industrious, and courageous," the Circassians were initially employed by the Ottoman authorities in the late nineteenth century to curb the restless Bedouin tribes along the desert line.[2] Alien settlers in the late nineteenth century, provoking antagonism among their Arab neighbors, the Circassians were gradually Arabized in language and culture, largely undergoing a process of assimilation. The Circassians established flourishing villages in northern Transjordan, such as in Amman—the nucleus of the future city and capital—in 1878 and in Jerash in 1884. Many Circassians later enlisted in the service of Emir (later King) Abdullah of Transjordan. Circassians played an important role in the "Arab Legion" (the army), including as officers.[3] Circassians have served in various government offices and in the cabinet, as well as engaging in several urban occupations. One prime minister, Sa'id al-Mufti, was a Circassian; he served as prime minister in four cabinets since the late 1940s. An element loyal to the regime, Circassians have also been overrepresented in proportion to their numbers in the lower house of the Jordanian parliament. In 1993, Tujan Faysal was the first Circassian (and radical) woman elected to the parliament, though she was not reelected in 1997. She acted by and large not as a representative of Circassian interests but rather as a Jordanian Arab, speaking for democracy, human rights, and social justice.

A political agenda similar to that of Tujan Faysal was presented by Emily Nafah, a Christian (and Communist) woman who ran unsuccessfully for one of the Christian seats in the 1997 parliamentary election.[4] Indeed, like the Circassians, Christians in Jordan have been loyal to the Hashemite Kingdom, overrepresented in parliament, and served as ministers in most cabinets. Largely integrated into the political and national society, Christians also play an important role in the economy. They have also continued to enjoy communal autonomy in matters of personal status and religious worship. Although Muslim–Christian tensions periodically flared in the Jordanian-held West Bank during the 1950s and early 1960s, Christians in the East Bank have rarely been mistreated by Islamic groups. On certain occasions Muslim and Christian politicians even formed electoral alliances against leftist candidates.[5]

In conclusion, the small Christian and Circassian communities in Jordan have been largely integrated into political and economic life as well as into the national community of the country. This is likely to continue as long as the monarchy maintains its strong control, its constitutional basis, and its process of democratization.

Notes

1. See Norman N. Lewis, *Nomads and Settlers in Syria and Jordan, 1800–1980* (Cambridge: Cambridge University Press, 1987), pp. 96, 107; and Onn Winckler, *Population Growth and Migration in Jordan* (Brighton, England: Sussex Academic Press, 1997), pp. 7–8.

2. Lewis, *Nomads and Settlers*, p. 11.

3. Ibid., p. 111; Mirza Basha Wasfi, *Kitab wathai'qi* (*Book of my documents*), (Amman: no date).

4. See Albert H. Hourani, *Minorities in the Arab World* (London: Oxford University Press, 1947), p. 59; *Area Handbook for the Hashemite Kingdom of Jordan* (Washington: U.S. Government Printing Office, 1974), p. 75. Saad Eddin Ibrahim, *Humum al-aqalliyyat: al-taqrir al-sanawi al-awwal* [*The Concerns of the Minorities: the First Annual Report 1993*] (Cairo: Ibn Khaldun Center, 1994), p. 209; Rami Khouri in *Jordan Times*, translated in *Ha'aretz* (in Hebrew), December 24, 1997; *Civil Society* 7, no. 77, May 1998, pp. 11–12.

5. See Naseer Hasan Aruri, *Jordan: A Study in Political Development, 1921–1965* (The Hague: Nijhoff, 1972), pp. 40–45; Sabah El-Said, *Between Pragmatism and Ideology: The Muslim Brotherhood in Jordan, 1989–1994*, Policy Paper no. 39 (Washington: The Washington Institute for Near East Policy, 1995), pp. 8–9.

Chapter 5

The Copts in Egypt: From Integration to Segregation?

As Egypt's largest minority, Orthodox Copts could have expected to experience a process of peaceful integration in their national community much like that which Jordan's Christians experienced. The Copts have ancient Egyptian origins, share a common social and cultural background with the Muslim majority, constitute a small percentage in the population (about 6 percent or some 4 million), and are involved to only a minor extent with foreign powers. Indeed, a process of integration did occur from the middle of the nineteenth century. But, as indicated in Chapter 1, this integration was periodically interrupted by militant Muslim action, causing Muslim–Christian tension and Coptic anxiety. Such swings of integration and rejection continued throughout the twentieth century. Generally speaking, during the quasidemocratic liberal period, the current of Coptic incorporation was more dominant, whereas under the authoritarian Egyptian regimes that have held power since 1952, the major trends have been rejection and segregation.

Under the 1923 constitution, all Egyptians, including the Copts, enjoyed equal civil and political rights. In the state institutions Copts served as ministers in all cabinets, as senators and deputies in all parliaments, and as civil servants in various ministries, and there was a high proportion of Copts in the private sector—businessmen, lawyers, engineers, pharmacists, physicians. Copts also became an integral part of the Egyptian national movement, notably within the major party, the Wafd, which was founded in 1919 and led by Sa'd Zaghlul. Makram Ubayd, a Copt, was "almost the dominant figure of the party."[1]

21

Under Mustafa Nahhas, Zaghlul's successor, a rift developed between himself and Ubayd and the latter withdrew from the Wafd, followed by most of the Wafd's Coptic members and supporters. The weakening of this secular liberal party, also owing to further splits, coincided with the rise in the 1940s of radical Islamic and Arab nationalist groups—notably the Muslim Brotherhood. In addition to engaging in occasional acts of anti-Coptic violence, the Muslim Brotherhood made an effort to restrict Coptic influence and economic and educational opportunities. The Egyptian government, influenced by the Muslim Brotherhood, issued regulations indirectly restricting Copts and other minorities from obtaining positions in the public administration and in foreign companies. The government also attempted to reduce the authority of the Coptic Communal Council (*Majlis Milli*), which had been legally recognized in 1915. Those government actions led a prominent Copt to conclude, in the 1940s, albeit perhaps with some exaggeration, "ever since, a systematic program has been under way to make Egypt a Muslim country and to exclude the Copts altogether from government, business, and education."[2]

During Gamal Abdel Nasser's revolutionary and authoritarian regime (1952–1970), Copts were further circumscribed politically and economically, and the state further encroached upon their communal institutions. Owing to the pan-Arab, military nature of the regime and its single party system, Coptic political participation was drastically diminished, notably in the cabinet, the National Assembly, and in most ministries, as well as in the legal, economic, and educational spheres. Similarly, more Copts than Muslims suffered financially as a result of Nasser's land reform and the nationalization of banks and businesses. The former measure, which applied to Waqf lands, also greatly reduced the income of the Coptic community, while the abolition of Christian (and also Muslim) religious courts seriously damaged the authority of the Coptic clergy. As a result of the various new measures, many thousands of Copts emigrated during the 1950s and the 1960s, and some who remained converted to Islam.[3] Yet, most Copts in Egypt were physically secure under Nasser's secular regime, for it severely repressed the Copts' greatest foe, the Muslim Brotherhood. Copts also expanded their communal religious, social, and cultural activities under the leadership of Patriarch Anba Kyrillos.

With the accession of President Anwar Sadat after Nasser's death in 1970, it seemed that the Copts were regaining their previous political and economic roles. Sadat was Egypt-oriented and promoted pro-Western policies and economic liberalization, replacing Nasser's pan-Arabism, Soviet alliance, and state socialism. Indeed, acknowledging the Copts' contribution to Egyptian civilization, Sadat appointed three Copts to the government, among them Fikry Makram Ubayd as deputy prime minister and Boutros Boutros Ghali as minister of state for foreign affairs. Gen. Fuad Ghali became the commander of the 2nd Egyptian Corps on the Suez Canal front during the October War in 1973, and several Copts were elected to parliament. Yet, many Copts considered these appointments as token gestures and complained about continued discrimination in the public sector, in higher education, in the legal system, and in building new places of worship.[4] In particular Copts became deeply worried, even alarmed (and Coptic students turned militant), in the face of the growing Islamization of the state. The strengthening of militant Islam in Egypt was manifested in acts of violence and even murder, particularly during the late 1970s[5] and under the influence of the Iranian Islamic revolution. Patriarch (or Pope) Shenuda and Copts in North America held public protests and lodged bitter—though occasionally exaggerated—complaints; these and other factors led Sadat to turn against Shenuda and the church, accusing them of creating a "state within a state." Sadat banished Shenuda to a monastery in Wadi Natrun[6] and then attempted to cultivate Coptic lay leaders to appease the community and to curb the Islamic militants. His assassination in 1981 by an Islamic extremist reflected the growing challenge or threat of radical Islam to both the Copts and the Egyptian government. Sadat's successor, President Hosni Mubarak, recalled Pope Shenuda from exile in 1985 and called for Muslim–Christian reconciliation, but Islamic militancy further increased.

In an attempt to undermine the system and challenge government policies, Muslim extremists periodically attacked state officials and foreign tourists. Particularly and most frequently they harassed and killed Copts,[7] burning down many churches, especially in southern Egypt, where Copts constitute about 20 percent of the population. In some cases Copts were attacked because they allegedly refused to pay the Islamic *jizya*.[8] In other cases, Muslim militants molested Muslim secular intellectuals and assassinated one—Faraj Fouda in 1992—because he had publicly denounced anti-Coptic actions. Although the security forces have managed since the mid-1990s to curb much of this Islamic violence, Copts feel no more secure than before. In addition to further Muslim attacks, Copts have continued to suffer from discrimination in certain state institutions, in the public sector, in education, and in the economic field. Copts have again become marginalized in political life, even though President Mubarak has declared time and again that the Copts are "an integral part" of the "national fabric." He has also allowed the construction of new churches and has endeavored to reduce anti-Coptic preaching in mosques. Shaykh Muhammad Tantawi, the leading Muslim religious authority, denounced "some terrorist groups trying to spread religious discrimination and hatred against 'Coptic citizens.'"[9]

Despite these statements and deeds, Copts have continued to emigrate from Egypt; reportedly two million had left by 1997. Of those who have stayed, some have converted to Islam, while many others have sought "refuge in self-protective isolation,"[10] or have adjusted to the grim conditions, hoping for future improvement.

In conclusion, President Mubarak is certainly concerned about the plight of the Copts, without fully acknowledging it; and thus may do more to improve their condition. But as long as he is unable to eliminate the Muslim militants and solve Egypt's serious socioeconomic problems, he will be unable to safeguard completely the Copts' physical security. Similarly, as long as the country maintains its Islamic character, and the domestic liberal, secular, and democratic groups remain small and uninfluential, Mubarak will be unable to restore the role of the Copts as full and equal members of Egypt's national and political communities. It is true that American Coptic associations and other Christian groups have been highly active in publishing and lobbying on behalf of the Egyptian Copts.[11] But effective American intervention on behalf of the Egyptian Copts is not likely to occur, because the Coptic problem in Egypt is confined within a fairly stable and strong state that is strategically important to the United States, and the problem carries no serious global or regional repercussions.

Notes

1. See Albert H. Hourani, *Minorities in the Arab World* (London: Oxford University Press, 1947), pp. 42–43, 47. On Makram Ubayd, see Mustafa al-Fiqi, *al-aqbat fi al-Siyasa al-misriyya* [*The Copts in Egyptian Politics*] (Cairo: Dar al-Shuruq, 1985). For more sources, see Yusuf Abu Sayf, *al-aqbat wal-qawmiyya al-arabiyya* [*The Copts and Arab Nationalism*] (Beirut: Markaz Diras at al-Wahdah al-Arabiyyah, 1987); Samira Bahr, *al-aqbat fi al-Hayat al-Siyasiyya* [*The Copts in Political Life*] (Cairo: Anglo Library, 1979), chapter 3; J. D. Pennington, "The Copts in Modern Egypt," *Middle Eastern Studies* vol. 18, no. 2 (April 1982), pp. 158-179.

2. Quoted in Edward Wakin, "The Copts in Egypt," *Middle Eastern Affairs* 12 (1961), p. 201.

3. Ibid., pp. 203–204; see also Moheb Zaki, *Civil Society and Democratization in Egypt, 1981–1994* (Cairo: Konrad Adenauer Stiftung, Ibn Khaldun Center, 1995), p. 202.

4. Pennington, "The Copts," pp. 168–174.

5. See Zaki, *Civil Society*, p. 197. See also Muhammad Hassanayn Haykal, *Kharif al-ghadab* [*Autumn of Fury*] (Beirut: Tawzi Sharikat al-Matbuat, 1983).

6. Zaki, *Civil* Society, pp. 196–197. Raymond A. Hinnebusch, *Egyptian Politics Under Sadat* (Boulder, Colo.: Lynne Rienner, 1985), p. 154. See Gilles Kepel, *Muslim Extremism in Egypt: The Prophet and Pharaoh* (Berkeley: University of California Press, 1995), pp. 205–208.

7. Kepel, *Muslim Extremism*, pp. 161–162; *al-Watan al-Arabi* no. 817, October 7, 1992, pp. 26–27. For full details, see *Humum al-aqalliyyat*

[*The Concerns of the Minorities*] (Cairo: Ibn Khaldun Center, 1993), pp. 39–45. See also Pennington, "The Copts," pp. 170–175.

8. See *al-Wasat*, no. 273, 1997, pp. 27–29; *al-Ahali*, March 19, 1997; *Middle East Report*, July–September 1996, pp. 21–23.

9. J. Danisjewski, "The Copts, Christians of Egypt," *Los Angeles Times*, July 24, 1997, pp. 7–8.

10. U.S. State Department, *Report on Religious Freedom in Egypt*, (Washington: U.S. State Department, July 22, 1997), p. 2; Zaki, *Civil* Society, pp. 200–205; *al-Watan al-Arabi*, no. 817, October 3, 1997, pp. 26–27.

11. For examples of publishing and lobbying efforts, see *Copts* magazine; the U.S. Copts homepage at http://home.netcom.com/~us_copts/; and the American Coptic Association and Christians of Egypt, information on which can be found at http://www.copts.com/.

Chapter 6

Arab Palestine
and the Jewish Community:
Upheavals in Intercommunal Relations

Christian–Muslim Relations

Like the Copts in Egypt, many Christians in Palestine—now divided among Greek Orthodox, Greek Catholic, and Latins (Roman Orthodox) as well as among several small denominations[1]—were already living in the area before the seventh century Arab Islamic conquest. They underwent a thorough process of Arabization and many of them—especially the peasants—also shared common customs with their Muslim neighbors. As indicated above, during the Ottoman period, Christians and Jews were tolerated and enjoyed communal autonomy, but they were treated as inferior subjects in the Muslim state, and in addition to the regular *jizya* (tribute), they were periodically forced to pay irregular taxes and fees. Their economic superiority, social seclusion, and communal–religious inequality occasionally exposed them to the contempt, jealousy, extortion, and violence of Muslim neighbors.[2]

During the mid-nineteenth century in particular, Christians in several towns suffered from Muslim oppression and aggressiveness in reaction to the equal status granted to them (and also to the Jews) by the Ottoman reformist government. Provoked by the Christians' quick and allegedly excessive exploitation of these non-Islamic reforms, and worried about the growing intervention of European powers on the Christians' behalf, many Muslims in Palestine developed feelings of suspicion, fear, and hatred, and they harrassed their Christian neighbors.[3] As a result, many Christians reinforced their religio–communal seclusion, and others emigrated.

A small but growing number of Christian Arab intellectuals, mainly Greek Orthodox, strove to create a common nonsectarian basis with their Muslim Arab compatriots, by working to revive the Arabic language and culture, introducing fresh patriotic and nationalist ideas, and stressing the potential common threat posed by the Jewish Zionist immigrants who began arriving in Palestine in the early 1880s. Christian Arabs indeed became leading figures in the pan-Arab, and later the Palestinian Arab, nationalist movement and in its political struggle against both the Zionist movement[4] and the British Mandate in Palestine (1920–1948). Some of them founded patriotic newspapers (such as *Falastin* and *al-Karmil*), organized national associations, such as the Muslim–Christian Association in 1918, and many more joined political parties in a desire to participate in and integrate into the emerging Palestinian national community.[5]

Like the Copts in Egypt, Christian Arabs in Palestine— some 10 percent of the total Arab population—naturally had more members and sympathizers in the quasisecular liberal parties, such as the Nashashibi faction, than in Islamic-oriented conservative organs like the Husayni faction.[6] As in the past, conservative Muslims remained suspicious, contemptuous, and jealous of the more prosperous and better-educated Christians. Occasionally, militant Muslims would criticize, threaten, and even harass Christians because of their overrepresentation in the public service and involvement in missionary activities, as well as their alleged disloyalty to the Arab cause.[7] But most Palestinian leaders, notably Hajj Amin al-Husayni, the mufti of Jerusalem, denounced anti-Christian actions and hailed Muslim–Christian unity. In particular these leaders praised the Christians' participation in national activities aimed at achieving Palestinian Arab independence and fighting the Jewish Zionist enterprise.[8]

In effect, the challenge of the growing Jewish Zionist minority—some 60,000 in 1917, reaching 600,000 by 1947—continued to be a major incentive for Christian–Muslim solidarity, particularly among the elites in the Palestinian national community.

Palestinian Arabs and Zionist Jews

Although representing the majority of the population—some 600,000 in 1917, reaching 1.3 million in 1947—and enjoying the backing of neighboring Arab states, the Palestinian Arab national community lagged far behind its Jewish Zionist opponents in motivation, organization, and performance. Indeed, rejected by East European and German Nazi anti-Semitism and motivated by their ancient national and historical attachment to Eretz Israel/Palestine, the Jewish *olim* (immigrants) created a powerful national community during the British Mandatory period. Initially and periodically backed by the British government, which in 1917 issued the Balfour Declaration favoring the creation of a Jewish national home in Palestine,[9] the Jewish *yishuv* (local community) constructed many villages and several towns in Palestine. It also established a modern and well-organized network of national institutions—political, economic, and educational—in addition to efficient paramilitary forces.[10]

The yishuv withstood or repelled Palestinian political pressure (largely exerted via the British), an economic boycott, and periodic guerrilla or terrorist attacks, while Jewish military organizations occasionally launched operations against Arabs. The Zionist movement obtained wide international sympathy and American Jewish support following the revelations of the Holocaust of World War II. The Zionists also benefited from the uncompromising positions of the Palestinians, who rejected the favorable British White Paper of 1939 as well as the United Nations (UN) partition resolution (181) of 1947.

The yishuv did accept this UN resolution and, although initially poorly equipped, its armed forces (the Labor-Zionist *Haganah* and the revisionist-Zionist *Irgun*) managed to repulse the attacks of irregular Palestinian and inter-Arab forces. After the proclamation of the State of Israel in May 1948, the newly organized Israeli army defeated several regular mili-

tary expeditions sent by Arab states in an attempt to abort
the creation of the Jewish state.

Jews, Israel, and the Minorities Problem in the Arab States

The success of the Jewish Zionist minority community in Palestine in achieving its major goal—creating a state in part of
the country—not only constituted a national calamity (*nakba*)
for the Palestinian Arab majority community; it also inflicted
a serious blow to pan-Arab ideology and to the policies of
Arab governments regarding the minorities problem in the
region. For a long time Arab ideology denied the national
rights of Jews and of other national minorities, and particularly the implementation of these rights in the Arab and
Muslim land of Palestine.[11] During the Mandatory period,
moderate Arab leaders were prepared to grant the Jews administrative autonomy only, in a small part of Palestine within
a Palestinian or pan-Arab (Greater Syrian) state.[12] But most
Arabs, including the Palestinians, preferred to treat the Jews
in Palestine as merely a religious minority, in accordance with
the Muslim tradition. Arab leaders rejected Israel on ideological grounds and feared its Zionist "imperialistic" nature,
but they were particularly worried that the success of the Jewish state would serve as a model for other minorities in the
Arab Middle East, encouraging them to follow suit and dismember the countries in which they lived.

As a matter of fact, in an attempt to repel the Arab siege
and hostility, and to foster a non-Arab, non-Muslim, pluralism
in the region, Israel at various times offered to help different
ethnic and religious minorities in Arab countries to achieve
their political objectives.[13] Before the establishment of Israel,
the Jewish yishuv had already maintained secret contacts with
Christian Maronite leaders in Lebanon. Following the creation
of the state, Israeli leaders toyed with notions of helping the
Lebanese Maronites to establish their own state in part of Lebanon (an idea of Ben Gurion's). This idea failed, however; as
Moshe Sharett said, he and his compatriots tried to "actively
assist any fermentation in the Maronite community aiming at
invigoration and detachment . . . as it may involve undermin-

ing stability, causing troubles to the [Arab] League, diverting attention from the Israeli–Arab complexity . . . and essentially rekindling the desire for Christian independence . . . but what can I do, such fermentation does not exist."[14]

From the mid-1970s to the mid-1980s during the Lebanese civil war, successive Israeli governments rendered military and logistical assistance to the Maronite Christians who, as Prime Minister Yitzhak Rabin said in 1976, "are struggling for their lives against the fanatic Muslim nationalist chauvinism" or, as Prime Minister Menachem Begin said in 1978, were allegedly facing "genocide" by the "fanatic" Muslims. Begin's government helped the Maronites not only to defend themselves against Muslim attacks but, in the 1982 invasion, also, in the words of Gen. Rafael Eytan, "to prevent the takeover of Lebanon by the Syrians and the [Palestinian] terrorists" and to reinforce pro-Israeli Maronite hegemony in Lebanon.[15]

Similar to their Maronite policy, since the 1930s Jewish Zionist leaders attempted to establish friendly relations with Druze chiefs in Lebanon and in Jabal Druz (the Druze Mount) in the Syrian region of Houran, with the help of the Druze in Palestine and then Israel. In late 1948 a senior Israeli Arabist in the Ministry of Foreign Affairs considered "that [a] connection with possible forces in Syria headed, of course, by the Druze, could create a lot of damage, stabbing a poisoned knife in the back of the Arab unity which remains intent on fighting us."[16]

Although the response of the Syrian Druze was not positive, during the June 1967 War, Minister of Labor Yigal Allon suggested occupying Jabal Druz and establishing an independent Druze state there, but the Israeli cabinet rejected the idea.[17] Similarly, according to Druze sources in the Golan, in the mid-1970s Israeli ministers Allon and Moshe Dayan tried in vain to persuade Druze leaders in the Golan Heights to accept the scheme of creating a buffer Druze state, stretching from Jabal Druz to the Golan Heights and Mt. Hermon, and reaching the Druze Shuf region in Lebanon.[18]

Israel has endeavored to help or conclude alliances not only with religious minorities living near its borders but also with ethnic groups fighting for self-determination in more remote areas. Thus from the early 1960s to the mid-1970s Israel supplied weapons and military training to the Kurdish rebels who fought under Mullah Mustafa Barazani against the Iraqi Arab government.[19] Since the late 1960s, Israel has periodically equipped and trained the southern Sudanese forces, *Anya Nya*, which launched guerrilla warfare against the Sudanese Arab authorities.[20]

Despite its efforts, Israel has been unable to implement fully its strategic objectives, as three of the above discussed minorities have so far failed in their struggle: the Kurds, the southern Sudanese and the Maronites. The Druze, as mentioned earlier, rejected Israeli initiatives and regarded themselves as Syrian or Lebanese Arabs, respectively.

It is worthwhile noting that, with one exception, there has been almost no public debate in Israel on its alliance with the various ethnic and religious minorities in the region, primarily because most connections with these minorities remained secret and unpublicized for many years. Israel's activities concerning the southern Sudanese rebels are still unknown to most Israelis, and its military relations with Iraqi Kurds have become public knowledge only in recent years, through a few publications,[21] but these have not incurred public debate. Similarly, there has been little information or discussion concerning Israel's connections with the Druze in Lebanon and Syria. Only its alliance with Lebanon's Maronites, particularly during the 1982 war, was widely debated and severely criticized by Israelis, for it followed the Maronite massacre of Palestinians in the Lebanese camps at Sabra and Shatila, as the Maronites attempted to drag Israel into the Lebanese quagmire.[22] It would appear that, following its involvement in Lebanon, Israel gradually terminated military relations with the minorities in the region except in southern Lebanon, instead placing a priority on creating peaceful coexistence with neighboring Arab nation states.

The next chapter will briefly examine the extent to which Israel's minorities strategy has affected its policy toward its own Arab minority.

Notes

1. On the various Christian communities in Palestine during the 1500s, see Amnon Cohen and Bernard Lewis, *Population and Revenue in the Towns of Palestine in the Sixteenth Century* (Princeton, N.J.: Princeton University Press, 1978). Concerning the period of the British Mandate, see Robert Brenton Betts, *Christians in the Arab East: A Political Study* (Athens, Lycabettus Press, 1975), pp. 66–67. See also Hassan bin Talal, *al-Masihiyya fi al-'alam al-Arabi* [*The Christians in the Arab World*] (Amman: Amman Library, 1995).

2. Uriel Heyd, *Ottoman Documents on Palestine, 1552–1615* (Oxford: Clarendon Press, 1960), pp. 174–175, 177, 181; Amnon Cohen, *Palestine in the 18th Century: Patterns of Government and Administration* (Jerusalem: Magnes Press, Hebrew University, 1973), p. 257; Dror Ze'evi, *An Ottoman Century: The District of Jerusalem in the 1600s* (Albany: State University of New York Press, 1996), pp. 22–23, 80.

3. See, for example, Moshe Ma'oz, *Ottoman Reform in Syria and Palestine, 1840–1861: The Impact of the Tanzimat on Politics and Society* (Oxford: Clarendon Press, 1968), pp. 187-199; Derek Hopwood, *The Russian Presence in Syria and Palestine, 1843–1914: Church and Politics in the Near East* (Oxford: Clarendon Press, 1969), pp. 46-67.

4. See Hopwood, *Russian Presence*, pp. 159–179; Neville J. Mandel, *The Arabs and Zionism Before World War I* (Berkeley: University of California Press, 1976). Prominent among the Christian Arabs in the pan-Arab and Palestinian nationalist movement were Khalil al-Sakakini, Najib Azouri, George Antonius, Ya'qub Farraj, Alfred Rock, and Emile al-Ghuri.

5. See Yehoshua Porath, *The Emergence of the Palestinian-Arab National Movement, 1918–1929* (Tel Aviv: Am Oved Publishers, 1976; in Hebrew), pp. 14–22; William B. Quandt, Fuad Jabber, and Ann Mosely Lesch, *The Politics of Palestinian Nationalism* (Berkeley: University of California Press, 1973); Rashid Khalidi, *Palestinian Identity: The Construction of Modern National Consciousness* (New York: Columbia University Press, 1997).

6. See Philip Mattar, *The Mufti of Jerusalem: Al Hajj Amin al-Husayni and the Palestinian National Movement* (New York: Columbia University Press, 1988), p. 70.

7. Yehoshua Porath, *The Palestinian Arab National Movement: From Riots to Rebellion, 1929–1939* (Tel Aviv: Am Oved Publishers, 1978; in Hebrew), pp. 137, 186, 211, 319–320.

8. Mattar, *The Mufti of Jerusalem*, pp. 70–71. On the Arab–Jewish struggle, see also J. C. Hurewitz, *The Struggle for Palestine* (New York: Schocken Books, 1976); Ahmad Tarabin, *Falastin fi Khutat al-Sahayuniyya wal-Isti'mar* [*Palestine in the Designs of Zionism and Colonialism*] (Cairo: Institute for Arab Research and Studies, 1976).

9. On the British role, see Hurewitz, *Struggle*; Aharon S. Kleiman, *Divide or Rule* (Jerusalem: Yad Yitzhak Ben-Zvi, 1983; in Hebrew).

10. For details, see Walter Laqueur, *A History of Zionism* (Tel Aviv: Shocken Publishing House, 1977; in Hebrew), pp. 262–264.

11. See "The Palestinian National Charter" in Walter Laqueur and Barry Rubin, eds., *The Israel–Arab Reader: A Documentary History of the Middle East Conflict* (New York: Penguin Books, 1984 [4th ed.]), pp. 366–372; Abdalla al-Hasan, *al-aqalliyyat fi al-waqi' al-Arabi* [*The Minorities in Arab Reality*] (Damascus: Mashriq-Maghrib, 1995); the Ba'th party constitution, 1947, quoted in Nikolaos van Dam, "Israel and Arab national integration: Pluralism versus Arabism," *Asian Affairs*, 10 (1979), p. 145.

12. See, for example, General Nuri al-Said, "Fertile Crescent Scheme, December 1942," in J. C. Hurewitz, ed., *Diplomacy in the Near and Middle East* (Princeton: D. Van Nostrand Company, 1965), vol. II, pp. 236–237.

13. Van Dam, "Israel," pp. 144–145.

14. Moshe Sharett, *Yoman Ishi* [*Personal Diary*], (Tel Aviv: *Ma'ariv* Library, 1978), vol. 8, pp. 2397–2400. See also Benny Morris, "Israel and the Lebanese Phalange: The Birth of a Relationship, 1948–1951," *Studies in Zionism*, 5 (1984), pp. 125-132. See also Patrick Seale's article in *al-Hayat* (in Arabic), April 20, 1998.

15. See Moshe Ma'oz, *Syria and Israel: From War to Peacemaking* (Oxford: Clarendon Press, 1995), pp. 167–175. See also Van Dam, "Israel," pp. 145–147.

16. Israel State Archives, Foreign Ministry 2570/11, Shimoni to Sasson, 16 September 1948, quoted in Kais M. Firro, *The Druzes in the Jewish State: A Brief History* (Boston: Brill, 1999), p. 79. See also idem, *A History of the Druzes* (New York: E. J. Brill, 1992), pp. 324–327.

17. Ma'oz, *Syria and Israel*, p. 102.

18. Tha'ir Abu Salih, "The political positions of the Druze in the Golan" (unpublished ms., December 1997, pp. 2–3; in Hebrew). Ghalib Abu-Muslih, *Al-Duruz fi zil al-ihtilal al-israili* [*The Druze in the Shadow of the Israeli Occupation*] (Beirut: al-'Irfan, 1975), pp. 247–249.

19. David Kimche, *The Last Option: After Nasser, Arafat, and Saddam Husayn, the Quest for Peace in the Middle East* (Tel Aviv: Hotza'at Adanim, 1992; in Hebrew), p. 200; Avner Yaniv, *Politics and Strategy in Israel* (Tel Aviv: Sifriyat Po'alim, 1994; in Hebrew), pp. 172–175. See also Mordechai Nisan, *Minorities in the Middle East: A History of Struggle and Self-Expression* (Jefferson, N.C.: McFarland, 1991), pp. 240–241; Mahmud 'Usman's article in *al-Wasat* (in Arabic), no. 298, October 1997, pp. 28–29.

20. See *al-Wasat* (in Arabic), no. 66, 1993; Yossi Melman, *Ha'aretz* (in Hebrew), July 1, 1997; Nisan, *Minorities*, p. 202.

21. Eliezer Tsafrir, *Ana Kurdi* [*I am a Kurd*], (Or Yehuda, Israel: Hed Arzi, 1999, in Hebrew)

22. Kirsten E. Schulze, *Israel's Covert Diplomacy in Lebanon* (New York: St. Martin's Press, 1998).

Chapter 7

The Arab Minority in Israel: From Segregation to Integration?

Israel's periodic endeavors to give help to non-Arab and non-Muslim minorities in the region have obviously been related to its bitter conflict with Arab–Muslim states and aimed at breaking up or unsettling these states while exposing their nondemocratic, nonpluralistic character. Israeli policy toward its own Arab minority was, for about two decades after 1948, similarly influenced by the conflict with the Arab nations. This minority was treated as an Arab "fifth column" and as such the state imposed strict restrictions on its members, incompatible though these restrictions were with Israel's declared liberal democratic nature. Only since the late 1960s, as Israel became stronger and began to feel more confident, did the state abrogate most of these restrictions and grant more equal civil and political rights to its Arab citizens. Nevertheless, it has never considered them as a national minority, but rather as separate religious communities that could adjust to or integrate into the Jewish state.

During and after the 1948 war, Israel's Arab population shrank dramatically through a tragic exodus, and over time it has moved from alienation to accommodation. Israel's Arabs did not revolt against their government, and only a small number have been involved in acts of sabotage or espionage. Recently, many have begun to acknowledge their long-delayed political rights and socioeconomic benefits. But while remaining basically loyal to Israel, they have been unable to identify with a Jewish Zionist state which by definition has not considered them as full and equal citizens.

In the Proclamation of Independence on May 14, 1948,

35

Israel was declared a "Jewish state," upholding the "full social and political equality of all its citizens, without distinction of religion, race or sex. . ." and called upon its Arab inhabitants "to play their part in the development of the State on the basis of full and equal citizenship."[1] But, born amidst a war launched by several Arab states, besieged and threatened, Israel was naturally apprehensive with regard to Arab intentions. It considered its Arab citizens (some 156,000 in 1949, out of some 800,000 people)[2] as an extension of its Arab enemies, and therefore a security risk. Two separate institutions were established to control them: a military government-cum-administration and an adviser on Arab affairs in the prime minister's office, and an Arab section of the General Security Service. Military government was imposed on three major zones comprising some 75 percent of the Arab population: the Galilee (in the North), the Triangle (East) and the Negev (South). Administered by strict emergency regulations and occasionally by arbitrary rules,[3] these were closed military zones where, for example, Arabs were required to obtain permits in order to travel to other parts of the country. Although it may have marginally contributed to safeguarding security, the military government was largely used for other purposes, such as appropriating Arab lands and increasing the Arab people's dependence on, or support of the ruling Jewish Zionist party Mapai (the Workers' Party of Eretz Israel).[4]

The humiliation, anger, or alienation felt by many Arabs because of these acts were intensified in late October 1956, during the Sinai–Suez War, as Israeli border police troops massacred forty-nine Arab villagers from Kfar Qasim in the eastern Triangle. Although the government condemned the massacre and the killers were (lightly) punished, many Arabs considered the incident a true reflection of entrenched anti-Arab positions among Israeli Jews.[5]

The military government was not abolished until ten years later, in late 1966, following strong criticism by various Israeli parties and associations. But the policy of preventing or thwarting the creation of independent Arab nationalist parties or groups (like the antistate group *al-Ard* in the early 1960s) continued for more years. Only the Israeli Communist Party—initially called Maki, then after 1965 Rakah, and now Hadash—with its Arab majority, freely represented political grievances and national aspirations. The *raison d'être* for this preventive policy was articulated in 1966 by the director of the Arab affairs department of Mapai: "There is a danger in the very existence of an Arab party that is not dependent on Jewish parties . . . a nationalistic [Arab] party which does not identify with the state is likely to bring about a disaster on the Arab community in Israel."[6] Further, as reported in 1962 by the security service: "The policy of the government has been to divide the Arab population into communities and areas . . . the sectarian policy and the clan divisions in the villages actively prevented the crystallization of the Arab population into one single entity."[7] Indeed, this Israeli strategy—which has gone on since 1948—was aimed at averting or obstructing the development of national cohesion and cultural identity among the Arabs by differentiating among various religious and ethnic communities and social groups, coopting the traditional elites, and influencing the education of the young generation.

For example, the Druze (some 10 percent of the Arab population) have been treated by Israel as non-Arabs, encouraged to develop their own communal "national" consciousness and pro-Israeli tendencies. The young men are mobilized for mandatory military service, special privileges are granted to the community, and a separate Druze curriculum is prepared for use in state schools.[8]

By and large, the Christian Arab communities—some 14 percent of the Arab population, mostly Greek Catholic (42 percent), Greek Orthodox (32 percent), or Latin (15 percent), as well as some Maronites and Protestants—have been treated with more respect than the Muslims. They have been encouraged to deal with their own religious matters and their young men are encouraged to volunteer for the Israeli army. In addition, the international affiliations of most Christian communities, as well as their high socioeconomic and educational levels, led the Israeli government to believe that they could be separated from their Muslim fellow Arabs. Muslim

Arabs—some 76 percent of the Arab minority—were until recently largely subject to stricter supervision, as they were regarded as an extension of the region's Muslim–Arab enemies.

Changes in Israeli Attitudes and in Arab Latitudes

Gradually, Israel has improved its attitude towards its Arab citizens, mainly owing to increased self-confidence and to the regional military superiority it acquired after 1967. These changes coincided with the replacement, in 1966, of David Ben Gurion's rigid policy toward Israeli Arabs with the more flexible positions of Prime Minister Levi Eshkol and some of his successors. Thus, while developing the infrastructure of many Arab villages, Israeli ministries, parties, and unions have admitted growing numbers of Arabs to their ranks. In addition to serving as Knesset (parliament) members—the most seats they have held thus far is 13 out of 120—several Arabs have served as deputy ministers, as members of the Knesset Committee for Foreign Affairs and Security, and as consuls, district judges, and senior officials; Israel has had one Arab ambassador and one Arab high court judge, and for the first time in 1999, a Muslim woman was elected to the Knesset.[9]

Summing up the improved socioeconomic and cultural conditions of Israeli Arabs, who constituted some 18 percent of Israel's population of 6 million in 1998, a Palestinian Arab scholar writes:

> The Arabs in Israel enjoy relatively high per capita incomes, by comparison with most Arabs in the Middle East region. They enjoy a relatively high level of education, for both males and females . . . the Arabs enjoy freedom of expression, religion, and social and cultural mobility, far beyond any degree of freedom enjoyed by any other community in the Middle East, except the Jewish majority in Israel. Israeli Arabs may attack government policy, hold public demonstrations, and criticize, publish against, or sue the authorities without fear of retribution on account of being Arabs.[10]

Indeed, Arab citizens have adopted the democratic and pluralist norms of Israeli society and, since the 1970s, have established several national parties and organizations consisting of modernized and self-aware Arabs—Muslims and Christians alike—who have struggled assertively for full political equality. Yet, this process of integration or "Israelization" of a growing number of Arabs has been marred by ongoing political inequalities and discriminatory legislation. Although there have been only a few cases of terrorism and sabotage, Muslims are often considered a security risk and are barred from holding nearly all sensitive or decision-making positions in the government and the state economy. They are discriminated against in the allocation of state lands and subsidies as well as in development projects, and a considerable number of Israeli Jews still refuse to consider them as full citizens. All these are obviously related to the inherent definition of Israel as a "Jewish state" or, since 1985, "the state of the Jewish people."[11] Although the vast majority of Arab citizens have been loyal to the State of Israel since 1948, many of them have been unable to identify with it fully, particularly on the emotional, cultural, and national levels.

Naturally, most of them have identified on these levels with their Palestinian brothers in the West Bank and Gaza, particularly since their reunion in 1967. This reunion contributed to the revival and enforcement of the current of "Palestinization" among Arabs in Israel, a current that has grown and been intensified by new developments or events. Among these, most notably, were the "Land Day" in March 1976, when six Arab citizens were killed by Israeli police while protesting against the confiscation of Arab lands; and the beginning in December 1987 of the Palestinian national popular uprising, or *intifada*, against the continued Israeli occupation of the West Bank and Gaza.

Alongside this Palestinian national current, an Islamic religious movement has also developed among Arabs in Israel, including among the Bedouin. This development followed the reunion with Muslim Palestinian groups and institutions—particularly in eastern Jerusalem—after 1967, and also took place under the influence of the Islamic revolution in Iran.[12]

This crucial dilemma of many Arabs in Israel, placed between their Palestinian national identity and their loyalty to the state in which they live, was partly and temporarily alleviated with the signing of the Oslo Declaration of Principles between Israel and the PLO in 1993. Israeli Arabs hoped that the conflict between their people and their state would be solved through a final settlement between Israel and the PLO, which most wish to include the creation of a Palestinian state in the West Bank and Gaza, and that they might provide a bridge of peace between Israel and the Arab nations.

Nevertheless, such a solution—which now, in August 1999, seems possible—could not in itself fully change what they view as their inferior status as an Arab minority in a Jewish state. For that reason, many Arab—and some Jewish—citizens have advocated not only the creation of a Palestinian state, but also the transformation of Israel from a Jewish ethnic state to a state of its citizens, where Arabs will have a fully equal status in a truly democratic country. The latter notion is totally unacceptable to most Israeli Jews, however, and they are also likely to reject an alternative idea, namely, to recognize the Arabs in Israel as a national minority and grant them collective rights ranging from sociocultural to political–territorial autonomy.[13] These Israeli–Jewish positions derive not only from a strong Jewish identity, but also from a lasting suspicion regarding the loyalty of Arab citizens to Israel. Many Israeli Jews fear that any autonomy granted to the Arabs in Israel will lead to an irredentist movement demanding annexation to a Palestinian West Bank entity or state. (A poll conducted in 1993 among Arabs in Israel showed that only some 10 percent of them sought to become part of a Palestinian entity, as against 26 percent who advocated integration within Israel; 22 percent preferred autonomy inside Israel, and 17 percent accepted the status quo.[14])

It can thus be surmised that the evolution of relations between Israel and its Arab citizens will be considerably linked to, or influenced by, the development in Israeli–Palestinian interrelations. A negotiated settlement between Israel and the PLO, one that currently looks as though it will include the establishment of a Palestinian state in the West Bank and

Gaza, would probably satisfy the great majority of Israel's Arab citizens and enhance their loyalty to the state, whereas only a fraction of them would possibly move to the new state. Large sections would rather act or strive by democratic political means to achieve cultural autonomy within Israel or to change its character to a state of all its citizens.

On the other hand, if the Palestinian problem is not settled in a mutually accepted way, and the bulk of Palestinians in the West Bank and Gaza launch a violent struggle against Israel, the Arab citizens of Israel—who are, of course, also Palestinians—are not likely to remain idle. Some of them would identify with their brothers in these territories, rendering them logistic, financial, and political assistance and embarking on public strikes and protests. Others might join their comrades in the territories in initiating militant operations—which in turn would provoke severe Israeli retaliation. All this would likely produce much bloodshed and perhaps lead to another Arab–Israeli war (as a worse case scenario), and it would certainly greatly damage Israel's relations with its Arab citizens and neighbors, as well as with the international community.

Theoretically, another way exists to resolve the relations between Palestinian Arabs and Israeli Jews, namely, to create in the whole of the land—including the West Bank and Gaza—a single state comprising both peoples and granting full and equal citizenship to all. But such a formula, which is advocated by not a few Palestinian Arabs, is totally unacceptable to the vast majority of Israeli Jews who wish to preserve the Jewish character of the state.

In sum, if Israel is to continue to be a state of the Jewish people and of its Arab citizens, and is to maintain its liberal democratic values, reaching a mutually acceptable agreement with the PLO over the "permanent status" of the West Bank and Gaza will be an important factor.

A Palestinian State and the Minority Problem

It may be hoped that a future Palestinian state would also have a vested interest in maintaining peaceful relations with

Israel for strategic and economic reasons and, under normal circumstances, that the state would not encourage irredentist tendencies among the Arab Palestinian minority of Israel.

Yet, the state would also have a minority "problem"; in the West Bank and Jerusalem, Palestinian Christians constituted about 8 percent of the population in 1967, though their numbers decreased to between 3 and 4 percent in the 1990s.[15] As for the status of this minority, a Palestinian state is likely to introduce full equality (at least in law) between the Muslim majority population and the Christian minority. This assumption is based on the various proclamations of the Palestinian national movement regarding equal rights for all, such as in the Declaration of Independence of November 15, 1988, by the Palestine National Council.[16] Moreover, in practice, Palestinian Christian Arabs in the West Bank, as in Israel, have for decades been strongly represented and actively involved on an equal footing in political parties, national associations, and guerrilla organizations. Significantly, many Christians, including church leaders, have participated in the struggle against Israel's occupation of the West Bank and Gaza, including the intifada.[17]

It is true that Islamic militants (even in Israel) have occasionally treated Palestinian Christians with suspicion and even violence; consequently, and owing to economic considerations, many Palestinian Christians have emigrated abroad. Yet, the longtime association of Muslims and Christians working together for Palestinian nationhood has been paramount and is likely to continue, especially among politicians, intellectuals, professionals, and the new middle classes. Thus, for example, a number of Christians have been elected to the institutions of the Palestinian Authority (PA) in Gaza and the West Bank, including seven to the Legislative Council (parliament)[18] and two to the Executive Authority (government). Symbolically also, PA chairman Yasir Arafat, a Muslim, in 1994 married Suha Tawil, a Christian who then converted to Islam.

In sum, neither the PA nor a future Palestinian state is likely to encounter any serious minority problems. Difficulties might emerge, however, if the Islamic militant movement

Hamas should take control and restrict Christian Arabs' political rights. Similarly, if certain Jewish settlements in the West Bank should be placed under Palestinian sovereignty within the final-status agreement, and if the residents face harassment by—or if they choose to disobey—the Palestinian authorities, minority relations could become an issue. Not only could such developments damage Palestinian–Israeli relations, but they could also disrupt the process of integration of the Arab minority in Israel. Some Israeli Jews fear that the creation of a Palestinian state could prompt some Israeli Arabs to develop irredentist tendencies toward their state. Generally, however, the bulk of Israel's Palestinian citizens are likely to strive for full equality within the state of Israel.

Notes

1. Walter Laqueur and Barry Rubin, eds., *The Israel–Arab Reader: A Documentary History of the Middle East Conflict* (New York: Penguin Books, 1995 [5th ed.]), pp. 107–109.

2. Jacob M. Landau, *The Arabs in Israel: A Political Study* (Tel Aviv: Ma'arachot, 1971, in Hebrew), p. 17. For more studies, see Sabri Jiryis, *The Arabs in Israel* (New York: Monthly Review Press, 1976); Fouzi Asmar, *To Be an Arab in Israel* (London: Frances Pinter, 1975); Habib Qawhaji, *al-Qissa al-kamila li-harakat al-Ard* (Jerusalem: al-Arabi Publications, 1978); Don Peretz, *Israel and the Palestinian Arabs* (Washington: Middle East Institute, 1958); Sammy Smooha, *Arabs and Jews in Israel* (Boulder, Colo.: Westview, 1989); Elia Zureik, *The Palestinians in Israel* (London: Routledge, 1979); Sarah Ozacky-Lazar, *The Crystallization of Mutual Relations between Jews and Arabs in the State of Israel* (unpublished Ph.D. thesis, Haifa University, 1996; in Hebrew), pp. 40–44.

3. For details, see Jiryis, *The Arabs in Israel,* chapter 1.

4. Dina Greitzer, *Ben Gurion, Mapai and the Attitude Towards the Arab Minority in Israel, 1948–1956* (unpublished Ph.D. thesis, Hebrew University, 1995; in Hebrew), Chapters 2–4.

5. Details in Jiryis, *The Arabs in Israel,* chapter 3.

6. Landau, *The Arabs in Israel,* p. 93.

7. Abba Hushi Archives (Haifa): Secret Report, "How to Treat the Arab Minority in Israel" (1962), cited in Kais M. Firro, *The Druzes in the Jewish State: A Brief History* (Boston: Brill, 1999), pp. 238–239.

8. For detailed studies, see Firro, *The Druzes in the Jewish State*; Gabriel Ben-Dor, *The Druzes in Israel: A Political Study* (Jerusalem: Magnes Press, 1979); Robert Benton Betts, *The Druze* (New Haven, Conn.: Yale University Press, 1988), pp. 101–107; Shakib Salih, *al-Druz wal-ta'rikh* [*The Druze and History*] (Haifa: Arab East Press, 1979).

9. See Aharon Layish, "Lines and Trends after the Six-Day War," in Aharon Layish, ed., *The Arabs in Israel* (Jerusalem: Magnes Press of Hebrew University, 1981; in Hebrew), pp. 241–247; Elie Rekhess, "Israel's Arab Citizens and the Peace Process," in Robert O. Freedman, ed., *Israel under Rabin* (Boulder, Colo.: Westview, 1995), pp. 189–204.

10. Elias H. Tuma, "The Arabs in Israel: Half a Century Later" (prepublication manuscript given to author in March 1998).

11. As'ad Ghanem, "State and Minority in Israel," *Ethnic and Racial Studies* 21 (1988), pp. 432–436; David Kretzmer, *The Legal Status of the Arabs in Israel* (Boulder, Colo: Westview, 1990), pp. 105–120. See Elie Rekhess, "The Arab Minority and the 1992 Election: Integration or Alienation," in Efraim Karsh and Gregory Mahler, eds., *Israel at the Crossroads* (London: St. Martin's, 1994), pp. 150–167.

12. Alisa Rubin Peled, "The Islamic Movement in Israel," in Hussin Mutalib and Taj ul-Islam Hashmi, eds., *Islam, Muslims and the Modern State: Case Studies of Muslims in Thirteen Countries* (New York: St. Martin's, 1994), pp. 278–297.

13. Yitzhak Reiter, "Between 'a Jewish State' and 'a State of its Residents,'" *Hamizrah Hehadash* 37 (1985), pp. 45–60 (in Hebrew). See also Claude Klein, *Israel as a Nation-State and the Problem of the Arab Minority—in Search of Status* (Tel Aviv: International Center for Peace in the Middle East, 1987), and Elie Rekhess, "Israel's Arab Citizens and the Peace Process."

14. Rekhess, "Israel's Arab Citizens," pp. 198–199.

15. See Daphne Tsimhoni, *Christian Communities in Jerusalem and the West Bank since 1948: An Historical, Social, and Political Study* (Westport, Conn.: Praeger, 1993), pp. 20–21.

16. Cited in Yehuda Lukacs, ed., *The Israeli–Palestinian Conflict: A Documentary Record* (Cambridge: Cambridge University Press, 1992), p. 413.

17. Tsimhoni, *Christian Communities*, pp. 8–9, 167–182; Betts, *Christians*, pp. 196–203.

18. Yvette Fayes, *Civil Society* (Cairo: Ibn Khaldun Center, July 1996), p. 14.

Chapter 8
Lebanon's Intercommunal Equilibrium: Its Emergence, Collapse, and Revival

U nlike the previous cases of minority–majority relations, in Lebanon a stable, if delicate, equilibrium existed for some decades among the several religious and ethnic communities, none of which constituted a clear majority. This multicommunal system collapsed in the civil war that began in 1975, but since the early 1990s it has been reinstated under Syrian authority, albeit with certain significant alterations. Interesting aspects, then, are mainly concerned with the factors and conditions that created and undermined this system, as well as with the prospects of its survival. To begin with, unlike most parts of the region, Mount Lebanon was inhabited for centuries mostly by Maronites and Druze and functioned as an autonomous *sanjaq* (district) within the Muslim-ruled Ottoman Empire. Although Christian Maronites formed the majority population in the Mount (some 60 percent, plus 25 percent Greek Catholics and Greek Orthodox), the minority Druze community, through its feudal lords, dominated the political and economic regime of Mount Lebanon.

Beginning in the late eighteenth century the Maronites underwent a process of educational and cultural development under the guidance of the Maronite church, economic growth outside the feudal regime, as well as administrative and political ascendancy with the help of the ruler, Emir Bashir II (1788–1840) who converted to Maronite Christianity. These developments coincided with and influenced the transformation of Druze–Maronite relations from feudal socioeconomic patronage to sectarian, religious-based political conflict.[1] The Druze, led by Shaykh Bashir Junblatt (1775–1825), succeeded in sustaining their communal cohesion and military supremacy but were unable to prevent the rise of the Maronites as a major political community imbued with religio–nationalist consciousness. Indeed, despite their military defeat by the Druze in the 1860 Lebanese civil war, the Maronites developed a national community in the autonomous Mount Lebanon that survived from 1861 to 1914 under international guarantees as well as continuous French political backing and cultural inspiration.

Once France assumed the role of a Mandatory power in Lebanon and Syria in 1920, the Maronites and Greek Catholics could have turned Mount Lebanon into a Lebanese–Christian polity. Yet, for strategic and economic considerations, many Maronites, led by their patriarch Huayk, worked to create a Greater Lebanon[2] that included large regions to the south, north, and east of the Mount—regions populated by many Sunni and Shi'i Muslims who intensely rejected this scheme.

Although their proportion in Greater Lebanon population diminished to 29 percent, the Maronites continued to exercise political predominance in the country, under French dominance. But French power and authority in the Levant eroded during World War II and as a new regional Arab alignment emerged. Influenced by economic calculations and Arab cultural inclinations, pragmatic Maronite leaders sought a power-sharing compromise with their Muslim fellow countrymen, notably the Sunni community, which constituted 21 percent of the population.

Thus, in 1943, a gentleman's agreement—the "National Covenant" (*al-Mithaq al-watani*)—was reached between Bishara al-Khuri, the new Maronite president, and Riyad al-Sulh, the Sunni prime minister, to shape Lebanon as a multicommunal Western democracy "with Arab features and Arabic tongue."[3] In accordance with the agreement, over the years Christian Maronites constantly occupied the most powerful position—the presidency—and Sunni Muslims held the second position in the hierarchy, that of prime minister. Other sects, which had not been consulted, accepted the agreement and were allocated less influential positions in the cabinet, parliament, and the government administration. The speaker, or president, of the parliament was to be a Shi'i Muslim, Shi'a Islam being the third largest religious community, with some 19 percent of the population. The various Christian and Muslim sects were to be represented in parliament in a ratio of six Christians to five Muslims, in accordance with their percentage in the population: 53 percent Christians (including Greek Orthodox at 10 percent, and Greek Catholics and Armenians, each at 6.3 percent) vis-à-vis 46 percent Muslims (including Druze at 6.3 percent of the population).

Yet, in the senior administrative, military, and economic positions, Christians—especially Maronites and Greek Catholics—and Sunni Muslims were in fact overrepresented, while Shi'is and Druze were underrepresented. The Shi'i communities, mostly in the South, were also economically and educationally underdeveloped and exploited by their feudal chiefs. The Druze, led by Kamal Junblatt, continued to show their historical antagonism to Maronite hegemony; conservative Muslims resented the new Christian predominance in Lebanon; and Muslim Arab nationalists disliked Lebanon's separation from Syria. At the other end of the spectrum, radical Maronite nationalists did not approve of the ideological and political compromise with the Muslims and continued to aspire to a smaller but Christian-dominated Lebanon.

Nevertheless, the new "confessional–consociational system seemed to be working splendidly . . . resting on a 'grand coalition' of sectarian and feudal–business 'notables.'"[4] It even survived a brief civil war in 1958 that evolved around Lebanon's regional Arab and global Western orientations, and which represented also a clash between two multisectarian groupings: one traditional, the other more modern. These groupings continued to compete for political influence, social patronage, and economic resources while fostering nepotism and corruption in state institutions.

Simultaneously, however, the existence of different educational networks, confessional parties and armed sectarian militias served to promote separate sectarian tendencies.

Moreover, the antiestablishment forces, namely secular antisectarian and socialist parties as well as Palestinian armed organizations, also grew stronger. Consisting primarily of nonprivileged Muslims, Shi'is, Sunnis, and also Druze, these radical forces were propelled by their own demographic growth, the strengthening of neighboring Arab states—notably Syria—and the intensification of Israeli attacks against Palestinian guerrillas in southern Lebanon.[5]

In the early 1970s, Interior Minister Kamal Junblatt—who himself headed the radical "Progressive Socialist Party"—permitted all these antiestablishment groups, including banned political parties, to operate legally. Subsequently, he organized several of these groups under his leadership in the "Lebanese National Movement." During the 1975–1976 phase of the civil war, employing his own Druze militia and concluding an alliance with the Palestine Liberation Organization (PLO), Junblatt emerged as the chief leader of the Lebanese radical—and mostly Muslim—opposition. His objectives were "to abolish the isolationist Maronite rule in Lebanon . . . the Crusader character . . . the political confessionalism—and to establish a secular democratic state."[6] (On another occasion, Junblatt reportedly said that the Maronites "have been governing us [the Druze] for 140 years and we want to get rid of them."[7])

Sunni political leaders hardly participated in the civil war. They were not interested in abolishing the system they shared with the Maronites, but rather sought to increase their part in it. Only several radical nationalist and militant religious Sunni groups, including an army faction, participated in the fighting against the Maronite-led system.[8] By the mid-1970s, the traditional Shi'i leaders had lost their political power to Musa al-Sadr, the new Shi'i *imam* (religious leader) of Lebanon. Born and educated in Iran, al-Sadr settled in Lebanon in the 1960s and in 1969 was elected head of the Supreme Islamic Shi'i Council of Lebanon. Subsequently, he created the popular Shi'i movement of the "disinherited" and demanded that the Shi'i community play a larger role in the political system and receive a greater share of economic resources.[9] With the outbreak of the civil war, al-Sadr established a Shi'i militia, *al-Amal* (Hope), which—owing to its alliance with Syria and the absence of strong anti-Maronite antagonism among its members—played only a marginal role in the fighting.

As for the Maronites, although their authority had been eroded and their leaders developed divergent interests and policies over the years, they shared a common objective: to protect the status quo and reinstate their hegemony. The three main Maronite leaders, Pierre Gemayel, Camille Chamoun and President Sulayman Franjiyya, joined forces and established the "Lebanese Front," which Chamoun headed. Their respective militias were unified in the "Lebanese Forces" under the command of Bashir Gemayel, Pierre's son. Many Maronite officers and their units sided with the Lebanese Forces. These forces, however, could not by themselves match the militarily superior radical alliance of Junblatt and the Palestinians.

The Maronites then simultaneously sought Syrian military intervention and Israeli military assistance. Syria, which had previously backed the Lebanese Muslim radicals and the PLO both ideologically and militarily, now became anxious lest this radical alliance assume control of Lebanon, become independent of Damascus, or provoke Israeli military intervention—or any combination of the three.[10] Consequently, in the summer of 1976, Syrian troops with Maronite cooperation fought and defeated the Junblatt–PLO military alliance. Damascus also engineered the election of Elias Sarkis, a bland pro-Syrian Maronite politician, as Lebanon's new president. Taking advantage of Syrian backing, Maronite militiamen massacred many Palestinians in the Tal al-Za'tar refugee camp in August 1976. In March 1977, Junblatt, the leader of the Lebanese National Movement, was assassinated—presumably by Syrian agents.

Subsequently, however, Syria made a rapprochement with the Lebanese radicals and with the PLO, and Maronite leaders, worried about the prolonged Syrian presence, sought Israeli help against Syria and its old–new radical allies.

As already indicated, Israel had for years maintained secret ties with Maronite leaders, aiming at sustaining the Christian character of Lebanon vis-à-vis its Muslim Arab environment. Reportedly, Israel extended military assistance to Chamoun's government during the 1958 crisis; and following the eruption of the 1975 civil war, the Labor government, under Prime Minister Yitzhak Rabin, supplied weapons to the Lebanese Forces to "help them to help themselves."[11] Following the ascendancy of the Likud in 1977, Prime Minister Menachem Begin expanded his government's direct involvement in Lebanon. Israel helped turn the Maronite-controlled militia in southern Lebanon into the "Southern Lebanese Army" (SLA) and committed itself to preventing an alleged "genocide" of Lebanon Christians by their "fanatic" Muslim enemy.[12] In June 1982, the Israeli army invaded Lebanon, ostensibly to eliminate the PLO infrastructure, but in practice also to oust the Syrian army and to install a pro-Israeli Maronite government in Beirut, according to the strategic design of Ariel Sharon, then Israel's defense minister.

Backed by Israel, the Maronite leader Bashir Gemayel was elected in August 1982 as president, but he was assassinated the following month, presumably by Syrian agents. The new president, Amin Gemayel, signed a the political agreement with Israeli in May 1983 but abrogated it in February 1984 under Syrian pressure. Subsequently, Syria managed to force Israeli troops out of Lebanon by means of guerrilla warfare by employing its proxies, especially the newly created Shi'i *Hizballah* (Party of God). Thus, except for the "security zone" in southern Lebanon, held by the SLA and the Israel Defense Forces, since 1985 Israel has ceased its military assistance to the Maronites in Lebanon, making Syria a clear winner in the struggle for Lebanon.

Yet, Syria needed five more years to terminate the civil war in Lebanon and to establish its hegemony there. Indeed, the internal conflict continued to be violent and was characterized not only by intersectarian warfare, but also by intrasectarian battles between rival Maronite militias as well as between the two Shi'i groups—Amal and Hizballah. The only militia that remained undivided was the Druze, under Kamal Junblatt's son Walid.

Damascus played the various militias and other forces, such as the PLO, against one another and used direct military strength, such as against the Maronite general Michel Aoun. Thus, Syria eventually managed to pacify Lebanon and impose a new political settlement. This was articulated in the Ta'if accord signed in Saudi Arabia in October 1989, designed on the basis of the 1976 constitutional reforms and approved by the Arab League and by the Lebanese parliament, under Syrian pressure. The new accord essentially reinstated the previous confessional system—as it was reflected in the 1943 national pact—but with significant changes, and with the intention to "abolish confessionalism in stages."[13] Accordingly, the president continued to be a Maronite Christian, but his powers were substantially reduced in favor of the Sunni prime minister and his cabinet. Greater authority and a longer term in office were granted to the Shi'i speaker of parliament (the Chamber of Deputies). In the new parliament and the civil service the six-to-five ratio of Christians to Muslims was changed to a fifty–fifty parity. In addition, the Ta'if accord provided for the disarmament of all sectarian militias and other guerrilla groups, while entrusting the Lebanese national army and security forces with safeguarding state security. Finally, depicting the Syrian army as "helping the Lebanese government to restore its authority," the Ta'if accord and the subsequent "Brotherhood and Cooperation Agreement" (May 1991) in fact gave Syria control over Lebanese national security and foreign policy.[14]

Thus, a major result of these agreements, and of the civil war, was the end of Maronite hegemony in Lebanon. Syrian troops brutally crushed Maronite General Aoun's attempt to maintain control in East Beirut in 1991. Earlier, in 1989, a pro-Syrian Maronite politician, Elias Hrawi, was elected president. After the assassination of president-elect Rene Muawwad in 1995, the Lebanese constitution was amended, under Syrian dictate, to extend Hrawi's term of office for an additional three years.[15]

Like Hrawi, other Maronites also adjusted to the new system, but many—led by the patriarch—resented it and boycotted the 1992 and 1996 elections. The traditional leading families were excluded or marginalized, for high emigration and a low birth rate had cost the Maronite community as a whole its initial demographic advantage, while collaboration with Israel had cost it its previous political prestige.[16]

In conclusion, the Maronites' chances for regaining their former hegemony in Lebanon would now seem very slim if not nil. Not only do they lack effective political and military power, they can no longer rely on outside intervention—from Israel, the United States, or France—to put them back in control. In Israel, the trauma of the 1982–1985 war in Lebanon still lingers and may prevent another major military intervention on the Maronites' side, unless a new war erupts between Israel and Syria over the Golan Heights or in Lebanon and a militant Israeli government decides to reactivate Ariel Sharon's 1982 strategy. The United States and France are not likely to press for a change in the new Lebanese system, or to work against either Syria's hegemony or its continued military presence in Lebanon. They would possibly urge the Maronites to integrate in the new system alongside other communities.

In contrast to the Maronites, the Sunnis, notably the new class of businessmen and politicians, have been the major beneficiaries of the post–civil war era. The Sunni prime minister—Rafiq al-Hariri from 1992 to 1998 and, since then, Salim al-Huss—was entrusted for the first time with substantial powers that at least match those of the Maronite president. Thanks to his successful economic projects and his Syrian backing, Hariri and his wealthy allies could also withstand the sociopolitical challenges of Lebanon's Sunni radical groups.

Unlike the Sunnis, many Druze were actively involved in the civil war and consequently developed high expectations regarding their share in future political and administrative systems. Yet, their part in the civil service remains small, and their principal leader, Walid Junblatt, has held only a secondary position in the government. Lacking the prestige and charisma of his late father, Walid has also been challenged by the rival Yazbaki faction, which includes Druze businessmen and intellectuals.[17]

Finally, the Shi'is—now the largest single community in Lebanon, constituting 30 percent to 35 percent of the population—have benefited from the postwar era more than the Druze but less than the Sunnis. The position of speaker of parliament, held by Shi'i leader Nabih Berri, has become more influential than ever before. Thanks to his close relations with Damascus and with both the Maronite president and the Sunni prime minister, Berri has become an integral part of the "troika" of Lebanon's leadership. Shi'is have also gained more prominence in the new army's officer corps, even though the socioeconomic conditions of many Shi'is have only partly improved. To gain political and economic ascendancy, the Shi'i community has a greater interest than any other group—except perhaps the Druze—in abolishing the sectarian system in Lebanon.[18]

Yet, the Shi'i community has suffered greatly from internal strife and competition between Berri's moderate secular Amal movement and the militant religious Hizballah. Hizballah is the only militia that has not been disarmed by Syria, so it can fight the SLA and the Israeli army in southern Lebanon. For its status as an armed militia, and owing to its extensive social activities and its links to revolutionary Iran, Hizballah has gained in popularity among Shi'is. With its ultimate goal of turning Lebanon into an Islamic state, however, Hizballah may in the future pose a serious challenge to the Lebanese political system as well as to Syrian hegemony. For example, in the event of an Israeli withdrawal from southern Lebanon as part of a Syrian–Israeli settlement, Hizballah may direct its energy and militancy toward gaining more power; it may perhaps also wage an armed struggle against the Syrian protectorate over Lebanon. In all likelihood, Damascus would be capable of handling such a challenge, not only through Lebanese and Syrian troops, but also by employing Amal and other sectarian forces to check Hizballah or by further integrating it into the political system. In any case, for the time being Hizballah has given up its grand Islamic design[19] and has participated in the parliamentary elections (winning twelve seats) as well as in the 1998 local elections, alongside other sects.

In this respect, the new Lebanese multisectarian system has reverted to the pre–civil war era. On the one hand, sectarian tendencies have remained high even among the younger generations of politicians, but on the other, alliances of Sunnis, Shi'is, Druze, and Christians have emerged in the parliament; and in the 1998 local elections more Maronites as well as members of other sects cast their votes.

In sum, it can be assumed that Syria may have an interest in maintaining the confessional system in Lebanon so as to maneuver among the various sects and leaders and to sustain its hegemony. But maintaining the multisectarian system in Lebanon runs counter to not only the 1989 Ta'if accord, but also the Ba'thist philosophy and policy of integrating all communities into one nonsectarian national community in Syria and in other Arab states. How Syria will overcome this contradiction remains to be seen.

Notes

1. For a detailed study, see Iliya F. Harik, *Politics and Change in a Traditional Society: Lebanon, 1711–1845* (Princeton, N.J.: Princeton University Press, 1968); or Antun Dahir al-Aqiqi (Malcolm H. Kerr, trans.), *Lebanon in the Last Years of Feudalism, 1840–1868* (Beirut: American University of Beirut, 1959).

2. See Meir Zamir, *The Formation of Modern Lebanon* (London: Croom Helm, 1985), chapter 2.

3. Theodor Hanf, *Coexistence in Wartime Lebanon: Decline of a State and Rise of a Nation* (London: I. B. Tauris, 1993), p. 72. For more studies on Lebanon, see Fahim Issa Qubain, *Crisis in Lebanon* (Washington: Middle East Institute, 1961); Kamal Salibi, *The Modern History of Lebanon* (London: Weidenfeld and Nicolson, 1965); Leonard Binder, ed., *Politics in Lebanon* (New York: John Wiley and Sons, 1966); Michael C. Hudson, *The Precarious Republic: Political Modernization in Lebanon* (New York: Random House, 1968).

4. Michael C. Hudson, "Trying Again: Power-Sharing in Post-Civil War Lebanon," *International Negotiations* 2 (1997), pp. 106–108. See Issam Nu'man in *al-Mustaqbal al-Arabi*, no. 63 (1984), pp. 54–71.

5. For details, see Hanf, *Coexistence,* pp. 141–143; Itamar Rabinovich, *The War for Lebanon, 1970–1983* (Ithaca, N.Y.: Cornell University Press, 1984), pp. 28–33. See also Halim Isber Barakat, *Lebanon in Strife: Student Preludes to the Civil War* (Austin: University of Texas Press, 1977); Adeed I. Dawisha, *Syria and the Lebanese Crisis* (New York: St. Martin's, 1980); Walid Khalidi, *Conflict and Violence in Lebanon: Confrontation in the Middle East* (Cambridge, Mass.: Harvard University Center for International Affairs, 1979); Tabitha Petran, *The Struggle over Lebanon* (New York: Monthly Review Press, 1987).

6. See Reuven Avi-Ran, *Syrian Involvement in Lebanon, 1975–1985* (Tel Aviv: Hotza'at "Ma'arakhot," Zva haganah le-Yisrael, Misrad ha-bitahon [Israel Defense Forces, Ministry of Defense], 1986; in Hebrew), pp. 39–40, quoting *al-Sayyad,* August 19–26, 1976.

7. See Rabinovich, *The War for Lebanon,* p. 200, quoting Asad's speech, July 20, 1976.

8. For details, see Rabinovich, *The War for Lebanon,* pp. 83–84.

9. See Fouad Ajami, *The Vanished Imam: Musa al-Sadr and the Shi'a in Lebanon* (Ithaca, N.Y.: Cornell University Press, 1986).

10. On Syrian policies and actions in Lebanon, see Dawisha, *Syria;* Avi Ran, *Syrian Involvement;* Rabinovich, *The War for Lebanon;* Moshe Ma'oz, *Syria and Israel: From War to Peacemaking* (Oxford: Clarendon Press, 1995), chapter 8.

11. See Ma'oz, *Syria and Israel,* pp. 160–168.

12. Ibid.

13. Text in *Tishrin,* October 24 1989.

14. See Hanf, *Coexistence,* pp. 583–585; see also Hudson, "Power-sharing," pp. 112–113. Text in *al-Anwar,* May 17, 1991.

15. See *al-Wasat,* no. 163 (1995), pp. 20–27; no. 171 (1995), pp. 10–17; no. 195 (1995), pp. 18–21; *al-Siyasa al-Duwaliyya,* no. 123 (1996), pp. 227–230.

16. See *al-Watan al-Arabi,* no. 835, March 5, 1993; no. 811, September 8, 1992; *al-Wasat,* no. 25 (1995), p. 7.

17. See *al-Wasat,* no. 166 (1995), pp. 17–18.

18. See *al-Wasat,* no. 157 (1995), pp. 30–31.

19. See *al-Watan al-Arabi,* no. 810, September 11, 1992; no. 833, February 19, 1993.

Chapter 9

Nonsectarian Nationalism in Syria: Obstacles and Achievements

Historical Background

Attempts at creating a nonsectarian national community in Syria had already begun a century before the ascendancy of the Ba'th regime. As mentioned in chapter 7, the outbursts in Damascus and Lebanon in 1860 intensified currents of emigration or isolation among many Christians but also prompted a number of intellectuals, mostly Orthodox and Protestant, to seek a new pattern of relationship with their Muslim neighbors. Aware of the dangers of religious sectarian loyalties and influenced by new European notions of secularism and patriotism, these Christian intellectuals introduced the concepts of *hubb al-watan* (love of the homeland) and *bilad Suriyya* (the land of Syria). They also endeavored to revive Arabic language and literature as another common denominator for a new nonsectarian Syrian society.[1]

Unfortunately, only a few Sunni Muslims and Druze embraced these new notions, whereas the majority population adhered to their respective religious sectarian and family–tribal affiliations. Thus, by the early twentieth century it was observed, by one contemporary Christian Arab Syrian intellectual, that "the patriotic bond [*irtibat watani*] is weak and is felt only by a few members of the upper class."[2]

It was only during the brief period of the semi-independent Syrian Arab state (1918–1920) that more systematic efforts were made to spread the ideas of nonsectarian patriotism and nationalism. Emir Faysal, the former military commander of the Muslim Arab revolt against the Turks who later became king of Syria and then Iraq, established himself in Damascus with the slogan *al-din li-'llahi 'wa'l watan li'ljami'* (religion is for God and the homeland for all).[3] Encouraging non-Muslims to participate in the Syrian Arab national community, Faysal also promoted Arabic language and culture as a basis of national identity. But his liberal policy toward non-Muslims (as well as toward the Jewish Zionist movement in Palestine) encountered severe criticism from most members of Syria's Congress, as they continued to stress the Islamic character of the state.

Faysal was unable to pursue his policy of national integration for any length of time. In July 1920 he was forcibly ousted from Syria by the French, who subsequently imposed a mandatory regime and fostered religious sectarian separatism by creating 'Alawi and Druze "states" in Jabal Ansariyya and Jabal Druze, respectively, by establishing a special administration in the Jazira region that was inhabited also by many non-Arab Christians and Kurds, and by bolstering religio–cultural autonomy among Christian (Arab) communities.[4]

The Syrian–Arab nationalist movement, while struggling against the French Mandate and for independence, endeavored to eliminate intercommunal cleavages and to forge a nonsectarian political community. Proclaiming religious freedom and tolerance, this movement included in its ranks not only Christians, some in senior positions, but also some Druze, 'Alawis, a few Jews and Arabized Kurds. Nevertheless, many conservative Muslim Arabs—notably the *'ulama* (religious leaders)—forced the nationalist government during the 1930s to avoid granting non-Muslims equality before the law.[5] At the same time, the bulk of the various minorities continued, with French backing, to maintain their communal autonomy and cohesion, while the Druze and 'Alawis adhered also to their armed centrifugal tendencies.

Changes since Independence

Once the French had gone in 1946, however, Syrian leaders were in a better position to embark upon the difficult task of achieving national integration. This process started on a large scale only under the military dictatorship of Adib Shishakli in the early 1950s, with attempts to Arabize the public institutions and the educational systems of all the communities. Shishakli also abolished the communal parliamentary representation that the various minorities had enjoyed under the French Mandate. A further step was to abrogate certain jurisdictional rights in matters of personal status, which had been granted earlier to the 'Alawis and the Druze. These new regulations, which sparked agitation among all the minority communities, were accompanied by a series of military measures designed to destroy the centrifugal forces of the Druze and the 'Alawis in the mountainous regions, and to establish a centralized rule in Damascus.

The crushing of the Druze revolt in 1954 became a turning point in the balance of power between the central government and the mountain-dwelling heterodox communities. For the first time, the authorities in Damascus were able to achieve a decisive military superiority over the rebellious minorities through the use of sophisticated weapons and methods. The seclusion and autonomy of those communities came to an end, and from then on they began to take an increasing part in political life and in the struggles for power in the army and between the parties. Following the precedent of their Christian compatriots, they began to join political parties, in particular those which stood for secularism and social change, such as the Syrian Nationalist Party (PPS) and the Ba'th; young members of the 'Alawi and Druze communities enlisted in the army in great numbers and consequently came to play an increasing part in Syrian politics.

Alongside this process, which went on during the 1950s and 1960s, other developments also contributed to drawing the minorities and other sections of the population closer to each other and planting the seeds of a common identity. These developments were the accelerated pace of modernization and secularization, and the intensification of national instruction through the expanding network of mass communication, notably the school system.

The state educational system expanded enormously after the end of the Mandate. The number of state schools grew from 658 in 1945 to 3,804 in 1964, whereas during the twenty years from 1925–1945 only about 300 new schools had opened. Over the same period the number of foreign and private (communal) schools diminished rapidly, decreasing—as a percentage of the total number of schools—from 40 percent in 1945 to 19 percent in 1951 to almost nil in 1967.[6]

Yet, during the 1950s and beyond, there was no consensus within the new political elite on the relation between state and religion in Syria. The 1950 draft constitution declared Islam as the state religion, but under pressure from liberal Muslims and from Christians the constitution stated that Islam is the religion of the Syrian head of state. The three modern parties that gained influence among the political and intellectual elites adopted the following lines: the PPS and the communists stood for Syrian secularism, and the Ba'th supported the separation of religion from state but considered Islam as a vital element in Arab nationalism. This position, combined with its pan-Arab ideology, made the Ba'th party more popular than its rivals.

Indeed, in the 1954 election, the Ba'th emerged as the third most numerous party in the parliament with 16 deputies out of 142. Within the army officers' corps too the Ba'th won the upper hand and managed to defeat successively the rival PPS (later the Syrian Socialist National Party, or SSNP) and communist factions. With the help of the veteran nationalist parties, the Ba'th led Syria into the historic union with Gamal Abdul Nasser's Egypt in 1958 to create the United Arab Republic (UAR). During this period, many Syrian officers were transferred to Egypt in an attempt to neutralize their power in Syria. But thirteen of these officers—mostly 'Alawis and Druze—established a secret "military committee" aimed at dissolving the union with Egypt and regaining Syria's independence under Ba'th leadership.

New Trends under the Ba'th Regime

The union with Egypt (1958–1961) was a highly traumatic experience for the Ba'thists and for many other Syrians, as they were barred from senior government and military positions and the country was under strict Egyptian control. This experience obviously contributed to reinforcing the concept of a Syrian–Arab nation-state among those officers and political activists who in 1963 became the backbone of the Ba'thist revolution and of its new authoritarian regime. This regime, headed until 1966 by Gen. Amin al-Hafiz, a Sunni Muslim, rested in practice on the support of the young 'Alawi and Druze officers who emerged in the 1966 coup as the new rulers of Syria. Subsequently, the 'Alawis ousted the Druze officers and later made further purges in the army. Led by Gen. Salah Jadid, the former chief of staff, and Hafiz al-Asad, the defense minister, and influenced by PPS–SSNP concepts and by Marxist ideas, these 'Alawi officers and their Sunni allies also carried out strict secularist and socialist reforms for the first time in Syria's modern history.

Their aim was to create a new Syrian national community composed predominantly of the lower and lower-middle classes: peasants and workers, army soldiers, public employees and the intelligentsia, and especially members of the younger generation. They established a strong authoritarian government and used the expanding state educational system, the media, and the Ba'th party to mobilize public support and to indoctrinate the people in the concepts of Arab nationalism, Syrian patriotism, socialism, and secularism, as well as anti-Zionism and anti-imperialism.

The neo-Ba'th regime succeeded in gaining the support of certain sectors of the population—mainly among peasants, workers, and the youth, and obviously in the 'Alawi community. Other sections of the population, however, especially the traditional middle and upper-middle classes—mostly Sunni Muslims as well as Christians and Druze—strongly opposed the Ba'th regime, particularly its secularist and socialist reforms, and deeply resented domination by a minority group of 'Alawi military officers.

Indeed, many Sunni Muslims in Syria considered the Ba'thist–'Alawi regime not only illegitimate and oppressive but also heretical and anti-Islamic. According to these people, especially the conservatives among them, the 'Alawi minority—a heterodox if not infidel sect, socially and culturally backward—had seized power in Syria by armed force, imposing harsh measures that severely hurt Muslim religious feelings and socioeconomic interests. For instance, in addition to the appropriation of land, banks, and middle-sized businesses, the Ba'th regime severely restricted religious education as well as the activities of the 'ulama, and attempted to weaken the Islamic character of the state. Thus, the new 1969 Syrian constitution omitted the clause declaring Islam to be the religion of the president. The wording of his oath was accordingly changed from "I swear by Allah Akbar" to "I swear by my honor and faith." The only reference to Islam was the vague phrase "Islamic jurisprudence is the chief source of legislation."[7] Led by 'ulama, conservative Muslims staged several violent protests and riots against the government. But these were brutally put down, in the process causing many deaths and the destruction of several mosques.[8]

Asad's Era

Well aware of the Sunni alienation brought about by Jadid's regime, Asad deposed Jadid in 1970 and adopted policies aimed at regaining the allegiance of the Sunni Muslim population and expanding the basis for the Syrian national community. This he did by changing or mitigating the measures of his predecessor, while promoting national patriotic unity and economic development. Regarding the Islamic issue, for example, in June 1971 Asad reinstated the presidential Islamic oath, lifted restrictions on Muslim institutions, encouraged the construction of new mosques, and improved the salaries and prestige of Muslim dignitaries. He also endeavored to underscore his own image as a faithful Muslim through a religious ruling from the Mufti of Damascus, as well as by other means.[9] At the same time, Asad's new regime introduced economic measures aimed at revitalizing small and middle-sized private enterprises (owned mostly by Sunnis), encouraging foreign investments, and expanding trade. It also used state organs to foster a popular consensus. In external affairs, Asad sought to improve Syria's relations with most Arab nations, notably Egypt, and to advance Arab unity by word and deed.[10]

Yet, during the 1970s and early 1980s, these efforts at nation-building encountered major obstacles and only partially achieved their goals. Like his Ba'thist predecessors, Asad's major failure lay in his inability to win the acquiescence, let alone the allegiance, of Sunni Muslim urban society, notably the conservative religious element. He failed not only because of the 'Alawi character of his military and security support base, but was because of the outcome of certain policies he adopted, which triggered furious Muslim reaction and ended in military repression.

Thus, for example, in early 1973 the "Islamic clause"—stipulating that Islam is the religion of the president—was deleted from the draft of the permanent Syrian constitution. This provoked violent Muslim disturbances and demonstrations in several towns against the "secularism and sectarianism" of the "fanatical 'Alawi regime," and against Asad, the "enemy of Allah."[11] Asad had these riots put down by an iron hand and with great loss of life, but he also reinstated the Islamic clause in the permanent Syrian constitution. A few years later, however, in 1976, Asad's military and political support of the Christian Maronites in their war against Lebanon's Muslim radicals provoked the Syrian Muslim Brotherhood into a fresh cycle of violent actions against the regime.

By the early 1980s these riots developed into an open Islamic rebellion against Asad's regime, fueled in part by economic difficulties that also stemmed from the Syrian involvement in Lebanon. In reaction, Asad authorized ferocious measures against the Muslim rebels and, in February 1982, Syrian military units shelled large parts of Hama—the center of the Islamic rebellion—killing between 10,000 and 30,000 people, including women and children.[12] This suppression of the Hama revolt undoubtedly neutralized the Islamic opposition to Asad's regime for a long period, but it also further alienated other Sunni Muslims, conservative and liberal alike.

Nevertheless, this terrible event apparently deepened Asad's awareness of the essential role of Islam and of the Muslim majority population in the construction of a Syrian national community. Consequently, since the late 1980s, he has revived and expanded his initial efforts to gain the allegiance, or at least to secure the acquiescence, of Sunni Muslims. He has continued to present himself as a good Muslim and has increased his gestures of goodwill toward Islamic institutions and the 'ulama. For example, many more mosques were built, new Qur'anic schools opened, Islamic cultural activities expanded, and women were again allowed to wear the *hijab* (traditional veil), which had been banned in the late 1960s. Further, a few thousand Muslim Brothers who had been jailed were released, while others who had fled abroad were allowed to return to Syria. Simultaneously, the regime—along with some "coopted" 'ulama—attempted to underline the pluralist and enlightened character of Islam in Syria.[13]

In this regard the regime has emphasized that the 'Alawis are an integral part of the Shi'a, that the Shi'is are closely associated with the Sunnis within the wider Islamic community, and that Islam is an essential element in the Syrian national community. Asad also took tangible steps toward integrating more Sunni Muslims into his regime and fostering their interest in its survival and success. Thus, large numbers of Sunni Muslims have been appointed or elected to various positions, including senior posts in the government, military, public service, parliament, the Ba'th party, and various professional and sectoral organizations.[14] Still, the military–security core—the intelligence networks, special forces, and major combat units—have been staffed mostly by 'Alawis or by non-'Alawis who are loyal to Asad.

It should be noted at this point that Asad's regime has adopted a policy of integration not only toward Sunni Muslims but also toward other Syrians, such as Christians and Druze, although not on a communal or religious basis. The domestic strategy of this regime has been to secure the allegiance of most Syrians, regardless of their religious affiliation, and especially the allegiance of the influential groups in the society, economy, army, and bureaucracy. The regime has pursued this goal by promoting the interests of various groups and linking them to the regime in a patron–client relationship. Most of these groups are professional, sectoral, or functional—such as the peasants' union, various trade and professional unions, the Chambers of Commerce and Industry, women's and youth associations, and the like. All of these organizations are structured hierarchically and are directly answerable to Asad or to his lieutenants.

Unlike previous Ba'thist rulers, who cultivated the public sector and advanced the lower classes of peasants and workers,[15] Asad has also encouraged the private sector and promoted the urban and rural middle and upper-middle classes—the new bourgeoisie. He has devoted special attention to productive economic factors in this sector, like the new business community and agricultural entrepreneurs. These groups have contributed to the national economy and have benefited from economic progress and from their close ties with the regime.[16] Many members of these new groups are Sunni Muslims, as are members of the traditional middle classes. (The traditional middle classes have also been encouraged to develop their private businesses.) These clusters, known as *al-Tabaqa al-Jadida* (the "new class") in Syrian society, have become a major element in Asad's support base, alongside the veteran support groups: the military, the bureaucracy, the party, and, obviously, the 'Alawi community. Most of these groups consist not only of members of the various religious and ethnic communities, but also of many lower-class people—rural and urban—who over the years have experienced a degree of socioeconomic or political mobility.

Asad has cultivated this fairly wide support base not only as a means of controlling—by way of patronage—the most influential sections of the population, but also to safeguard his regime. By amassing such a wide base of support, Asad has managed to blur his regime's authoritarian and minority character, while highlighting its pluralist and nonsectarian nature, and presenting the regime as a focus of the new Syrian national community.

The crucial question is: To what extent has Asad succeeded in achieving these goals, specifically that of creating a nonsectarian national community? It is obviously too early to give a definite answer regarding this long-term process, as it has been periodically interrupted by sectarian conflicts. Yet, there is no doubt that Asad's authoritarian minority rule has managed to achieve unprecedented political stability in Syria by means of stick-and-carrot tactics, employing on the one hand instruments of coercion and on the other supplying socio-economic benefits and political participation to core groups in the population, regardless of their religious affiliations.

Stability in a country previously torn by conflict probably could not have been attained without Asad's brutal measures and his qualities as a strong leader and shrewd politician. Most notable are his firmness, pragmatism, and patience, as well as his ability to learn from his mistakes. These qualities, together with his policy of creating an infrastructure of national institutions, have contributed to consolidating a strong and fairly wide basis for a national community.

Undoubtedly, many Syrians, particularly Sunni Muslims, have passively accepted or adjusted to Asad's 29-year-old regime and see no better alternative to it, including an Islamic regime. Many Syrians, born and raised in the independent state of Syria and under Ba'th rule, have probably developed Syrian Arab national patriotic feelings. They have also been influenced by their state education, and by seeing their country's transformation under Asad's rule into a more modern state and regional power.

True, some sizable groups remain latently antagonistic to Asad's regime, namely, traditional middle class Sunnis who continue to resent rule by the 'Alawi minority; liberal professionals who oppose the regime's repressive measures; and the urban proletariat and poor *fellahin* (peasants), who suffer economic hardship. But most of these groups either are disorganized or are partly neutralized by economic benefits or police control.

On the other hand, growing sections of the population—including Sunni Muslims in the urban and rural middle and upper classes—are perhaps satisfied with Asad's rule, thanks to their socioeconomic progress and political mobility. Several respect Asad's leadership and some do not consider the 'Alawis as usurpers of power, but as an integral component of the Syrian national community. A growing number of Sunnis have indeed established political and economic as well as social and marital links with 'Alawis, particularly those who have moved to urban centers and have been integrated into the socioeconomic fabric.[17]

As for the position of the non-Arab ethnic minorities in the Syrian national community: five of these are rather small communities. Christian Armenians constitute only 4 percent, as many Armenians emigrated in the 1960s; most Assyrians and Jews emigrated in the mid 1990s; Sunni Muslim Circassians account for only 0.75 percent of the population; and Turkomans also make up less than one percent. Each of the minority groups that has remained has been at least partly Arabized and has integrated into, or adjusted to, the Syrian state. This is also the case for some Kurds—the largest non-Arab, Sunni Muslim ethnic minority, at about 7 percent of the population. The veteran urban Kurds in particular, who constitute 10 percent to 15 percent of the Kurdish population of Syria, have largely assimilated. But many among the tribal and rural Kurds in the Jazira region and north of Aleppo have been periodically subjected since the 1950s to harsh measures aimed at suppressing their ethnic identity, such as forced Arabization, bans on the use of the Kurdish language and schooling, state sanctioned discrimination, and, for certain groups, forced transfer to other regions of Syria and denial of Syrian citizenship.[18] Yet, these severe measures have not provoked major violent reactions among the Kurds in Syria, in Iraq, or even in Turkey (whose militant organization, the PKK—Kurdistan Workers' Party—has used Syrian territory since 1984 as a base for guerrilla attacks on Turkish troops and installations). In any case, the Kurds in Syria are not likely to disrupt Asad's strategy of internal unity.

In conclusion, during Asad's rule, an increasing number of Syrian Arabs—Sunnis, 'Alawis, Christians, and Druze—have participated in a process of national integration whose main components have been the ideas of Arab nationalism, Syrian patriotism, and nonsectarian unity. This process has been augmented by political stability, economic improvement with a new capitalist orientation, and limited socio–religious pluralism. These trends toward the creation of a nation-state or national community are likely to persist in Asad's lifetime— and perhaps even after his death, provided that the 'Alawi–Sunni elite alliance is maintained.

Notes

1. See for example *Nafir Suriyya* (Beirut) October 25, 1860; see also Albert H. Hourani, *Arabic Thought in the Liberal Age, 1798–1939* (London: Oxford University Press, 1962), pp. 101, 274–277.

2. Yusuf al-Hakim, *Suriyya wa'd-ahd al-'uthmani* [*Syria and the Ottoman Era*] (Beirut: Dar al-Nahar, 1966; in Arabic) vol. I, p. 84.

3. Sati al-Husri, *Yawm Maysalun* [The Day of Maysalun] (Beirut: Kashaf Library, 1947), p. 77.

4. See Albert H. Hourani, *Syria and Lebanon: A Political Essay* (London: Oxford University Press, 1946), pp. 93–95; Philip S. Khoury, *Syria and the French Mandate: The Politics of Arab Nationalism, 1920–1945* (Princeton, N.J.: Princeton University Press, 1987), pp. 71–77.

5. See League of Nations, Permanent Mandate Commission 27th Session (1935); Albert H. Hourani, *Minorities in the Arab World* (London: Oxford University Press, 1947), p. 77.

6. See Rizkallah Hilan, *Culture et developpement en Syrie et dans les pays retardés* [*Culture and Development in Syria and the Developing World*] (Paris: Éditions Anthropos, 1969; in French), pp. 286–295; *al-Jadid* (Beirut), September 29, 1967; *al-Ba'th* (Damascus), October 12, 1967.

7. *Al-Thawra* (Damascus), May 3, 1969.

8. Abdul Latif Tibawi, *A Modern History of Syria, including Lebanon and Palestine* (New York: St. Martin's Press, 1969), pp. 415–417; Eric Rouleau, "The Syrian Enigma: What is the Baath?" *New Left Review* 45 (1967), p. 64; *al-Hayat* (Beirut), May 5, 1967; *al-Nahar* (Beirut), May 9, 1967. See also Nikolaos Van Dam, *The Struggle for Power in Syria: Sectarianism, Regionalism, and Tribalism in Politics, 1961–1978* (London: Croom Helm, 1979), pp. 104–105.

9. Moshe Ma'oz, *Asad, the Sphinx of Damascus: A Political Biography* (London & New York: Weidenfeld and Nicholson, 1988), pp. 150–151.

10. Ma'oz, *Asad*, pp. 74–82, 109–115. Patrick Seale, *Asad of Syria: The Struggle for the Middle East* (London: I. B. Tauris, 1988), pp. 169–177.

11. Ma'oz, "The Emergence of Modern Syria," in Moshe Ma'oz and Avner Yaniv, eds., *Syria Under Assad* (New York: St. Martin's Press, 1986), p. 32.

12. Ma'oz, *Asad*, pp. 159–163; Seale, *Assad*, pp. 320–338.

13. Ibrahim Hamidi, *al-Wasat* (London), May 13, 1996; Ibrahim Hamidi, *al-Wasat* (London), June 3, 1996; Hasan Sabra, *al-Shira* (Beirut), December 11 1995; *al-Sabil* (Jordan), June 21, 1996.

14. Raymond A. Hinnebusch, "Asad's Syria and the New World Order," *Middle East Policy* 11 (1993), pp. 11–12.

15. For a comprehensive survey and analysis, see Raymond A. Hinnebusch, *Peasant and Bureaucracy in Ba'thist Syria: The Political Economy of Rural Development* (Boulder, Colo.: Westview, 1989).

16. See *al-Hayat* (London), September 5, 1995 and July 2, 1994; *Die Zeit*, September 15, 1995; Volker Perthes, *The Political Economy of Syria under Asad* (New York: I. B. Tauris, 1995), pp. 109–122; *al-Thawra* (Damascus) June 2, 6, 9, 1990; *Financial Times*, May 10, 1994.

17. See Perthes, *Political Economy*, p. 122.

18. *Human Rights Watch* (newsletter), vol. 8, no. 4(c) (October 1996).

Chapter 10

Ethnic and Religious Conflicts in Iraq

U nlike the Ba'th 'Alawi minority rule in Syria that has had to cope mainly with the Sunni majority, the Ba'th Sunni minority regime in Iraq has been confronted with two major challenges: a Shi'i majority community (more than 50 percent of the population) and a sizable Kurdish ethnic minority (some 20 percent). Iraq's complex demographic religious, sectarian, and ethnic conditions are compounded by its geographic location—bordering on Shi'i Iran, with its Kurdish minority, and with the Kurdish region of Turkey. Add to this the topography of the Kurdish region in Iraq, the militant nature of Kurdish nationalism and of Shi'i radicalism, as well as the periodic involvement of external powers, and it may be concluded that of all the states in the Middle East, Iraq, under the Ba'th as well as during previous regimes, has encountered perhaps the hardest obstacles in its attempts to create a national community.

The first moves toward national integration occurred soon after the creation in 1920 of the Iraqi state and the accession in 1921 of Faysal I as the country's first king. Possibly repeating his previous endeavors in Syria, Faysal tried to advance the notions of nonsectarian Arab nationalism and Iraqi patriotism through public education and cooption into state institutions. The Iraqi cabinets and parliaments, for example, included Shi'is, Kurds, Christians, and Jews and other small minorities, such as the Turkomans, Persians, Yazidis, and Assyrians.

The constitution of 1925 guaranteed all minorities equality before the law, civil and political rights, and, if their language or religion—or both—differed from that of the majority, freedom in those realms as well.[1] Small minorities like the Jews and the Arab Christians tended to integrate into the new Iraqi state. For example, as one of the ancient communities in the land, Jews were represented by one cabinet minister and four parliamentary deputies; they also played a major role in Iraq's economic, political and cultural life. For a while, during the 1920s and early 1930s, members of the Jewish elite considered themselves as Iraqi–Arab nationals of Jewish religious beliefs.[2] But after the end of the British mandate in 1930 and the death in 1933 of the liberal-minded King Faysal, the position of the Jewish community—as well as those of other minorities—suffered a serious setback. These problems were the result of the emerging instability in the state and the intervention of the military in politics, as well as growing militant Arab nationalism in Iraq.[3]

As far as the Jews were concerned, their setback was also caused by the impact of fascist ideas and anti-Zionist tendencies (in response to the Zionist Palestinian conflict) among Iraqi Arab youth. Despite occasional government attempts to protect them, Jews periodically suffered harassment and violence, and several were murdered by Arab nationalists. In June 1941, about 180 Jews, including women and children, were massacred in Baghdad during the notorious *farhud* (pogrom).[4] Finally, the 1948 Arab–Israeli war in Palestine again provoked harsh anti-Jewish measures, now also taken by the government, including many imprisonments and a few executions. (In later years, notably in the late 1960s, more Iraqi Jews were executed for "spying" for Israel.) The majority of Iraq's Jews emigrated, most to Israel, leaving behind many assets.

Unlike the Jews, who endeavored to integrate into the Iraqi state and did not pose any threat to it, the non-Arab Christian Assyrians whom the British settled in Northern Iraq after World War I sought full autonomy or even a "national home" in their region.[5] Previously recruited and armed by the British, the Assyrian special troops refused to disarm after Iraq's independence in 1930 and allegedly threatened the national unity. In early August 1933, armed Assyrians clashed with Iraqi troops and, in retaliation, Iraqi and Kurdish military units massacred hundreds of unarmed Assyrians. Many other Assyrians fled the country.

Other small minorities, like the Turkomans and Yazidis, did not pose any crucial problem to the state but were, nonetheless, occasionally persecuted by the authorities or their Arab neighbors. The formidable Kurdish minority in the North and the Shi'i Arab majority community, mostly in the South, however, have continued to be the major challenges to Iraqi national unity.

The Shi'i Challenge

For many generations before Iraq's independence, most of the region's Shi'is lived in tribal formations in what is now southern and central Iraq.[6] Underdeveloped and oppressed by the Sunni authorities of the Ottoman Empire because of the religious schism, they were suspicious and resentful of the Sunnis. Upon the creation of Iraq, however, Shi'is and Sunnis joined forces in the 1920 uprising against British rule. And although during the reign of King Faysal Shi'i *mujtahids* (religious leaders) continued to adhere to the idea of a Shi'i state, their political influence was curbed by the government, which also adopted harsh measures against the Shi'i Iranian clergy in Iraq. On the other hand, Iraqi governments coopted many Shi'i tribal leaders by means of economic benefits and political appointments, mainly as members of parliament. Simultaneously, a growing number of Shi'is in search of work moved to urban centers, particularly Baghdad, and were exposed to the notions of Arabism and Iraqi patriotism, mainly through state education. Many of them joined, or were influenced by, all-Iraqi political parties, including socialist and secular ones, and they consequently became more detached from Shi'i religious identity. Over the years, more and more Shi'is were enrolled in government and public employment while some held ministerial positions, including that of prime minister.

Yet, the Shi'i leadership demanded half the ministerial positions in every government, an equal share in the civil service including the army officer corps, and an equal share in the allocation of government resources. They also objected to the pan-Arab nature of Iraqi national ideology at the expense of Iraqi Arabism.[7] While King Faysal was in power, he managed to appease the Shi'is somewhat by gestures and promises. But after his death, political instability and growing incitement by Sunni opposition leaders encouraged the Shi'i tribes to resort in 1935 to antigovernment demonstrations and other acts of defiance. These acts included a series of uprisings in the middle Euphrates region and in the South that were put down by the Iraqi army and air force.

A positive result of the demonstrations was an increased representation of Shi'i tribal chiefs in parliament, but Shi'i calls for parity with the Sunnis in the government and the civil service remained unanswered. This setback was largely caused by conflicting interests among the various Shi'i sections and the lack of a strong political leader who could represent the entire community.[8] (The government thwarted the attempts of the mujtahids to fill such positions.) Nevertheless, various Shi'i ministers—among them prime minister Salih Jabir (1947)—ventured to recruit members of their community to senior government positions, causing Sunni suspicion and resentment and reinforcing the Shi'i–Sunni divide. Significantly, in 1951, Jabir's popular socialist party became for the first time a predominantly Shi'i party, but the Sunni politicians, headed by Nuri Said, managed—with the army's backing—to outmaneuver Jabir and his Shi'i followers. Frustrated by their exclusion from full political participation and socioeconomic mobility, many young and educated Shi'is were attracted to the Communist Party, its concepts of equality among Iraqi communities and classes, and its opposition to incorporating Iraq in pan-Arab unions.

At the same time, the adherence of young Shi'is to Communism also reflected a rebellion against the mujtahids' authority and thus unintentionally contributed to the revival of the role of Najaf and Karbala, the holy Shi'i cities, as centers of anticommunist orientation and Shi'i religious radicalism. Both these trends were substantially strengthened following the 1958 Iraqi revolution, which General 'Abd al-Karim Qasim led, with the help of his communist allies.[9] In 1960, Shi'i religious leaders formed the *Da'wa al-Islamiyya* (Islamic Call), with the goal of combating the alleged procommunist, anti-Islamic regime of Qasim, and of establishing an Islamic state in Iraq.[10] Led by Muhammad Baqir al-Sadr, a prominent Shi'i scholar, the Da'wa attracted not only poor Shi'i migrants in urban centers, but also growing numbers of young and educated Shi'is who were disappointed by the successive revolutionary rulers of the republic, starting with Qasim (1958–1963), continuing with the Arif brothers (1963–1968), and culminating with the Ba'thist governments. Apart from their non-Islamic, quasi-secular policies, these various regimes alienated many Shi'is because of their Sunni dominance or their pan-Arab orientations—or both—as well as their brutal repressive measures against Shi'i religious leaders. Such measures included the execution of Baqir al-Sadr in 1980 along with other Shi'i religious leaders and hundreds of other Shi'is; the arrest, torture, and deportation of a great many members of the Da'wa or of other newly formed Shi'i radical organizations such as the *Fatimiyah* group (1964) and *al-Mujahidun* (the Muslim Warriors, 1979).

Undoubtedly, the radical Iraqi Shi'is' main source of inspiration was the Iranian leader, Ayatollah Ruhollah Khomeini, who was exiled from Iran in 1964. He lived in Najaf and briefly in Paris, in 1978, before he became the leader of the Islamic Shi'i revolutionary regime in Iran in 1979. The latter event provided devout Iraqi Shi'is with a catalyst for anti-Ba'thist protests and guerrilla attacks, and it served as a model for their would-be Islamic state in Iraq. Even so, many Iraqi Shi'is have continued to feel allegiance to the Iraqi Arab state and have rejected the notion of a merger with Islamic Iran, but they have had to struggle to achieve greater representation, if not a Shi'i hegemony, in Iraq.[11] This allegiance to Iraq was evident during the long Iraq–Iran War (1980–1988), when most Iraqi Shi'i soldiers remained loyal to their state and did not defect to the Iranian lines, also partly out of fear of retribution by the regime.

During Operation Desert Storm in 1991, when a U.S.-led allied force defeated the Iraqi army following the latter's invasion of Kuwait, armed Shi'i rebellions erupted in southern Iraq, partly owing to American and Iranian incitement. These uprisings were accompanied by the execution or flight of many government and Ba'th party officials and brought about temporary Shi'i control in several towns, including Najaf and Karbala. In addition, Iranian-trained Iraqi Shi'is, organized by the Supreme Assembly of the Islamic Revolution in Iraq (SAIRI) under the leadership of Muhammad Baqir al-Hakim, also joined the rebellion in southern Iraq. Yet, on the whole, the Shi'i revolt was unorganized and lacked both a definite religious leadership and a clear political goal, except for that of overthrowing Saddam Husayn's regime. Indeed, given the American and inter-Arab objection to the dismemberment of Iraq and the ultimate military superiority of the Iraqi army, it was highly unlikely that the rebels would be capable of, or have a goal of, creating a Shi'i state in southern Iraq, let alone in the whole of the country.

In fact, the large Shi'i population in Baghdad did not join the uprising, if only for fear of Saddam's Republican Guard, which after a few weeks managed to crush the rebellion and reestablish government control in southern Iraq while draining the marshes there to facilitate military movements.

While Saddam demolished large sections of the holy Shi'i cities of Najaf and Karbala, including some shrines and libraries, and arrested or evicted most Shi'i clergy and religious scholars, he also considerably revived his previous endeavors to accommodate most other Shi'is in the Iraqi state. Saddam was greatly active in integrating the Shi'is in Iraq by means of political participation, socioeconomic benefits, and state education, but efforts had also been made—if not as vigorously—before Saddam's ascendancy. For example, General Qasim, who led the 1958 revolution, was of Shi'i–Kurdish descent, and he was assisted in the revolution by two Shi'i officers. Subsequently, Qasim appointed a Shi'i and a Kurd to a three-member sovereignty council which also included a Sunni Arab as the state president. Two Shi'is also served as ministers in his cabinet, while other Shi'is held various positions in the army and in government ministries.[12]

Similarly, under the rule of Abd al-Rahman Arif, from 1966 to 1968, a Shi'i senior officer, Naji Talib, served as prime minister for almost a year, and another Shi'i held the position of deputy prime minister, alongside three other deputies. Many Shi'is continued to move to urban centers, especially to Baghdad, and to occupy positions in the civil service. Yet, a large number of middle and upper class Shi'is in the private sector lost much of their wealth after the government implemented the land reform laws and nationalized private companies, Furthermore, Shi'is still received less education than Sunnis, generally speaking.

During the rule of the Ba'th party (in 1963 and since 1968), and particularly under Saddam's leadership, an unprecedented number of Shi'is were coopted in the party, the state, and society. Two of the initial founders of the Ba'th party in Iraq in 1948 were Shi'is—Fuad al-Rikabi and Sa'dun Hamadi. When Rikabi served as a member of the Ba'th command, from 1950 until 1963, and as the party's first secretary (1952), the number of Shi'is in the party and its regional leadership grew fairly high: some 54 percent of the party was Shi'i between 1952 and 1963.[13] This growth was largely due to Rikabi's effective recruitment efforts in Shi'i areas. In 1958, he served as the only Ba'thist minister in Qasim's government, but he resigned in 1959 and was later ousted from the party. Between late 1963 and 1970, representation of Shi'is in the Ba'th leadership dropped to 14 percent, although during the 1963 rule of the Ba'th, Shi'is were the leaders of two out of the three rival Ba'thi factions. Between 1968 and 1980, Shi'is again increased their representation in the Ba'th and state leadership—in 1977 reaching 28 percent in the Revolutionary Command Council (RCC), the highest decision-making institution; 26 percent in the Regional Leadership (RL) of the party—the second most important institution; and 25 percent in the government.[14] By 1987 the figures were 33 percent in the RCC, 30 percent in the RL and in the government. In addition, 50 percent of the members of parliament were Shi'is, although only 13 percent of the army officers were (even though most soldiers were Shi'is). Following Operation Desert Storm and the Shi'i rebellion, the number of Shi'is in the national and provincial leadership was drastically reduced, but later it gradually increased again, particularly in lower positions, including in southern Iraq.[15]

It would thus appear that since the Ba'th era began in 1968, and especially since Saddam took power in 1979, Shi'is have become increasingly integrated into Iraq's political fabric, state institutions, and economy, but they are still underrepresented in senior positions in the government, the Ba'th party, the officer corps, and the security network. Indeed, the reins of power continue to be held by the Arab–Sunni minority, notably by Saddam and his relatives, alongside a growing number of Sunni Arab tribal groups. This Sunni Arab disposition certainly reflects Saddam's suspicions and concerns regarding Shi'i loyalty. It also indicates the continuing Sunni–Shi'i tension in Ba'thi Iraq. Nevertheless, while maintaining tight control in Shi'i populated areas, Saddam has also endeavored, both before and after 1991, to mitigate this tension, appease Shi'i conservative circles, and absorb more and more young Shi'is into an Iraqi Arab national community. To this end he has not only used state education and economic development in Shi'i areas, but has also attempted to forge a common Iraqi heritage and ethos. Highlighting for awhile the ancient Mesopotamian civilizations as the early origins of all Iraqis,[16] Saddam has largely stressed the common values of Arab nationalism and culture, the unique role of Iraq in Arab and Islamic history, and the special bond between Shi'i and Sunni Arabs in Iraq. His endeavors to revive a Sunni–Shi'i alliance in Arab Iraq will probably be increased in future years in face of the non-Arab Kurdish secessionist movement.

Although it is impossible to evaluate accurately the impact of Saddam's ideological indoctrination, political security measures, and socioeconomic policies on the Shi'is of Iraq, the following conclusions may nevertheless be reached:

- A great many Iraqi Shi'is, while rejecting Saddam's policies, are unwilling (and unable) to create a separate Shi'i state in Iraq or to merge with Shi'i Iran.
- Most Shi'is consider themselves Iraqis, or Iraqi Arabs, and wish to secure a larger share in the government and state resources, in accordance with their demographic strength.

- The chances of a successful radical Shi'i religious ascendancy in Iraq are rather slim if not nil.

This leaves the Iraqi state to tackle the more formidable Kurdish challenge.

Kurdish Nationalism and Separatism

Modern Kurdish nationalism emerged in the region[17] for the first time around 1910, largely in the reaction of some intellectuals to the harsh regime of the Ottoman Young Turks. At the end of World War I, a Kurdish tribal leader, Shaykh Mahmud Barazanji, attempted to establish a Kurdish entity under the protection of Great Britain and possibly with its encouragement. The British, who had conquered Iraq during the war and sought to maintain their hold in this oil-rich region, made promises, along with France, to the Kurds at the 1920 Sévrès Conference, namely, to create an autonomous Kurdish entity, with an option for subsequent independence in a large section of the former Ottoman Kurdistan, including parts of present-day eastern Turkey and Northern Iraq.

In 1922, the Iraqi Kurds, unlike their counterparts in Turkey, were granted by the British the right to establish a government in their populated areas.[18] But rather than permitting the Kurds to implement this right, the British later helped the Iraqis to quell the insurrections that broke out periodically under the leadership of Barazanji. New circumstances and calculations had prompted the British to forgo their commitment to the Kurds: Under the 1923 Lausanne Treaty the former Ottoman Kurdistan was divided among the newly formed states of Turkey, Iraq, and Syria; many other Kurds lived in Iran and some in the new postrevolutionary Russian state.

In 1932 and again in 1944, the independent Iraqi monarchy pledged to grant the Kurds cultural autonomy and a share in the government administration in their region. In fact, the Iraqi government, while coopting groups of mostly urban Kurds and nominating some of them to senior state positions, tried gradually to Arabize the Kurdish region. In reaction, the Kurds renewed their rebellion during 1943–1946 under the leadership of Shaykh Mustafa Barzani. But the internal tribal divisions among the Kurds helped the Iraqi government (with the aid of Britain's Royal Air Force) to put down the uprising. Barzani and his comrades fled to Iran and he served as a senior officer in the newly created, Soviet-engineered Kurdish republic of Mahabad (1946).[19] With the collapse of that republic, Barzani moved to the Soviet Union, staying there until 1958, when he was permitted by the new Iraqi republican regime to return home.

At this point, it is worthwhile recalling the main factors and issues that shaped or influenced Kurdish relations with the Iraqi governments during both the monarchical and republican regimes. While seldom demanding full independence, the Kurdish nationalists continuously asked for political–territorial or administrative autonomy in their region, as well as a proper representation in state institutions and a share of the oil revenues in Kurdistan. Occasionally they suggested establishing an Arab–Kurdish federal, democratic system in Iraq that would answer to their wishes. Most Iraqi governments obviously rejected the demands for Kurdish territorial autonomy, let alone independence, and refused to grant the Kurds a proportional share in the central government and in state resources. Yet, several governments attempted to absorb "loyal" Kurds, especially those who lived in Baghdad, into the state institutions. Most Iraqi governments during the republican era would promise, often under Kurdish military pressure, to recognize Kurdish cultural and national rights and to grant the Kurds administrative autonomy in certain areas and within a countrywide decentralized system. Subsequently, however, these governments would avoid implementing those pledges fully or even partly, while instead fostering internal Kurdish disputes and attempting to advance their own control in Kurdish areas. The Kurds, for their part, used their topographical advantage, their fighting spirit, and periodic external support to launch armed rebellions and make further political demands.

Although most Kurdish tribes managed to join forces over a long period under the leadership of Mustafa Barzani and his

Kurdish Democratic Party (KDP), which he established in 1946,[20] the chronic intra-Kurdish rivalries have caused serious setbacks in the national struggle. Other obstructions have been created by various external powers who either opposed Kurdish independence or, under changing circumstances, ceased to support the national movement. Apart from the British, who stopped backing the Iraqi Kurds in the mid-1920s, Turkey and Iran agreed with Iraq (in the Sa'dabad pact of 1937 and the Baghdad Pact of 1955) to curtail inter-Kurdish activities between their respective countries. The Soviets dropped their support of the Kurdish republic of Mahabad in return for economic transactions with Iran, but they hosted Mustafa Barzani in Russia until the 1958 revolution in Iraq. The USSR obviously welcomed the General Qasim's new Iraqi regime and hailed its rapprochement with the Kurds, but after the late 1960s, the Soviets gave preference to their relations with Baghdad over their backing of the Kurds.

Indeed, during the early years of Qasim's rule, Kurdish–Arab relations in Iraq seemed to be flourishing for the first time in the twentieth century. The new provisional constitution of Iraq stated that "Arabs and Kurds are equal partners in this nation and state, and the constitution guarantees the national rights of the Kurds within the Iraqi national entity."[21] General Qasim also nominated a Kurd (alongside a Shi'i and a Sunni Arab) to a three-member sovereignty council as a symbol of Iraqi national unity. He appointed other Kurds to senior government positions, including one minister. But he refused to grant the Kurds national or political autonomy in Kurdistan. Consequently, after a brief period of collaboration, the Kurdish nationalists under Barzani's leadership renewed their rebellion, defeated several Iraqi army expeditions, and subsequently established in the Kurdish mountains a de facto autonomous government, as well as a strong military force.

This military included Kurdish army officers who had defected from the Iraqi army. The troops were also trained and equipped in the early- to mid-1960s by Israeli experts who traveled to Kurdistan via Iranian territory.[22] Subsequently and until 1975, this strong Kurdish entity, assisted also by Iran and the United States, played a crucial role in domestic Iraqi politics, owing to its effect on the regime's stability.

Thus, while the Kurds continued to demand regional political autonomy in Northern Iraq, the successive Iraqi governments that formed after Qasim's downfall offered them several plans for political settlement, amidst periods of armed clashes.[23] The first plan the Kurds accepted was the twelve-point program of Prime Minister Abd al-Rahman Bazzaz in June 1966 (during the revolutionary leadership of the Arif brothers). It recognized, among other things, Kurdish nationality and national rights within Iraq, and provided for Kurd representation in the parliament and the government in proportion to their population. It also promised them autonomous powers in fields such as administration, education, and health in their areas on the basis of a decentralized system.[24] But the Ba'th government that seized power in 1968 refused to implement this agreement and attempted to pit the Kurdish faction led by Jalal Talabani, as well as other tribes, against Barzani's leadership.

Following further armed clashes and bloodshed, an agreement based partly on Bazzaz's plan was signed in March 1970 between Mustafa Barzani and the Ba'thist government. For the first time, it provided for *hukm dhati* (political–territorial autonomy or self-rule) in the Kurdish populated areas of Iraq, except for the oil-rich Kirkuk region, whose future status would be determined in a referendum. In addition, it stipulated that a Kurd would be appointed vice president and five Kurds as cabinet ministers. It also declared that the Iraqi nation is composed of mainly two peoples: Arabs and Kurds.[25] But this agreement was not fully implemented, owing to unilateral steps taken by both parties. The Ba'th government, in particular, attempted to undermine Barzani's position, and even to assassinate him, as well as to settle more Arabs in Kurdish areas, notably Kirkuk. While demanding further concessions from Iraq, the Kurds asked for and obtained more military and financial assistance from Iran and the United States.[26]

In April 1974, the Kurds resumed their war, but within a short time the Iraqi army succeeded in occupying large

Kurdish territories, including the cities of Kirkuk, Irbil, and Sulaimaniyya. Indeed, at that time, Iraq was better prepared to meet the Kurdish military challenge. It had gained more political stability and financial resources after nationalizing the oil industry, as well as better Soviet weapons following the Soviet–Iraqi agreement of 1972. Yet, to overcome the powerful Kurdish forces in their mountainous strongholds, Iraq had to make Iran stop supporting the Kurds and discontinue American and Israeli military aid to them via its territory. Baghdad was prepared even to recompense Tehran with a historic concession—Shatt al-Arab, the waterway leading to the Persian (Arab) Gulf. This agreement was signed in March 1975 in Algiers and shortly afterwards the Kurdish rebellion collapsed. Barzani escaped to Iran, then moved to the United States where he died in 1979. Mustafa Barzani's son, Masud, was then elected as the KDP chairman, but he was faced with a hostile splinter faction, the PUK (the Popular or Patriotic Union of Kurdistan), which had formed in June 1975 under the leadership of Jalal Talabani. While Barzani's KDP revived its guerrilla warfare against Iraq and created a military alliance with revolutionary Iran, the PUK, which was initially backed by Syria, made a rapprochement with the Iraqi government in the early years of the Iraq–Iran War (1980–1988).

Saddam Husayn, Iraq's strongman since the early 1970s and president since 1979, adopted severe measures against the Kurds, which in fact constituted a genocide. Large-scale executions, deportations and relocations were carried out, as was the demolition of all the Kurdish villages along the border with Iran.[27] Simultaneously, however, he implemented the autonomy plan for the Kurds, under strict control, and allocated considerable sums of money for economic and social development in the Kurdish areas, playing off the rivalry between Jalal Talabani and Masud Barzani. In 1983 he entrusted Talabani and his PUK with the tasks of running the autonomy and fighting against the Barzani–Iranian military alliance.

But before long Talabani lost faith in Baghdad's Kurdish policy and by the mid-1980s he joined forces with Barzani in a newly established "Iraqi Kurdistan Front" (IKF), backed by

Iran. This "front" intensified guerrilla attacks, alongside Iranian assaults, against the Iraqi Army. In retaliation, the Iraqi Army viciously attacked Kurdish areas, using, among other things, chemical weapons—as in the notorious case of Halabja in 1988—killing many thousands of Kurds, including women and children, deporting many others, and destroying scores of villages.[28]

During the war, Turkey cooperated with Iraq against the Kurdish rebels in both countries, while the United States, the USSR, and France helped Iraq in its confrontation with Iran. But when the 1991 war broke out over Kuwait, the United States organized an anti-Saddam military coalition that included European and Arab countries as well as Turkey. The United States called upon the Kurds, as well as the Shi'is and Iraqis in general, to revolt against Saddam, but Washington did not actually help them fight the Iraqi Army. Moreover, the one-time Kurdish–Shi'i cooperation during the war proved short-lived. Following the ceasefire with Iraq, the United States and its allies did not prevent the Iraqi troops from further crushing the Kurdish rebellion with immense savagery, causing the flight of 1.5 million Kurds.[29]

Still, after prohibiting Iraq to move troops into, and fly over, the Kurdish region north of the thirty-sixth parallel (the so-called "safe haven"), the United States extended humanitarian assistance to the Kurds and helped them to establish their government institutions in Irbil. The CIA, in addition, was assigned to establish headquarters for the Iraqi opposition groups (the Iraqi National Congress) and to train Kurdish commandos to help topple Saddam's rule. Yet, under no circumstances has the United States been prepared to support the creation of a separate Kurdish state in Iraqi Kurdistan, mainly because of the following considerations: (1) it has not wanted to commit either troops or an ongoing political involvement in Kurdistan; (2) it has wished to avoid alienating its Turkish allies who have vehemently opposed a Kurdish state in Northern Iraq, lest the new state serve as a model for the Kurds in Turkey; and (3) it has not been inclined to rebuff its Arab allies who, ideologically and patriotically, opposed the dismemberment of Iraq as an Arab state. In sum, Washington intended to use the Kurdish region—while safeguarding it against Baghdad's aggression—to topple Saddam, but without dismantling Iraq or creating a Kurdish state.

Turkey started direct negotiations with the Iraqi Kurds for the first time in March 1991, aiming primarily at preventing them from creating an independent state. In return for its logistic help, including oil supplies, Turkey asked the Kurds to reject the Iranian influence in their region and to help Turkey fight the guerrillas of Abdullah Ocalan's Kurdistan Workers' Party (PKK). The Iraqi Kurdish leaders accepted Turkey's terms, assuring it that they "did not want to establish an independent state in Northern Iraq . . . our goal is to establish a federation of Arabs, Turkomans, and Kurds [in Iraq]."[30] Under those circumstances, in 1992 the Kurdish leaders Barzani and Talabani established a de facto autonomous government in Irbil, which included an elected legislative council and other institutions. Both factions shared power in a fifty–fifty ratio, while Barzani and Talabani served as copresidents of the IKF. Alas, the long and deep rivalry between the two leaders and their factions became a major liability in the attempt of the Kurdish national movement to create an autonomous entity or state in Northern Iraq. In addition to their differences in tribal and social affiliations, dialects, and Sufi order adherences, both factions compete for supreme authority and for control of revenues, especially on goods imported from Turkey. These bitter disputes have not only been exploited by Turkey, Iran, and Syria, and certainly Iraq, but have also led Barzani and Talabani periodically to strike alliances with these powers to gain an advantage over each other, while sacrificing Kurdish national goals and gains as well as many lives.

Indeed, since late 1994, several armed clashes have broken out between the two factions, claiming many casualties and causing great destruction.[31] Only the intervention and mediation of various Western governments, notably the United States, have periodically produced ceasefire agreements, political cooperation, and administrative reforms. But the continued rivalry has seriously undermined Kurdish solidarity while enhancing the intervention of hostile powers. Thus, for example, in late 1994 Talabani's armed militia, now backed by Iran, seized the Kurdish parliament in Irbil by force and occupied the entire city in late 1995. In August 1996, Barzani's faction, backed by Turkey and directly helped by Iraqi troops, overpowered Talabani's PUK, in Irbil and Sulaymaniyya, but in October 1996 he was repulsed from the latter city by Talabani and his Iranian allies.[32]

Taking advantage of the August 1996 battle over Irbil, Iraqi troops crushed the anti-Saddam opposition, the Iraqi National Congress. The troops also shattered the U.S. Central Intelligence Agency station in Irbil, which had organized and financed this "congress." But after America launched warning air attacks in southern Iraq, the Iraqi troops withdrew from Irbil and another fragile ceasefire was reinstated. Since then, the United States has revived its efforts to mend fences with Barzani and again to forge an agreement between him and Talabani.[33] In mid-September 1998, the two Kurdish leaders reached in Washington a new accord to share power and economic resources in Iraqi Kurdistan.[34] This in line with renewed American endeavors to support the Iraqi opposition and to topple Saddam's regime.

Whether or not this agreement becomes effective, the future status of Iraqi Kurdistan largely depends on the positions and policies of Turkey, Iran, Iraq, and the United States. The United States may again protect this region against Iraqi threats but it remains unwilling to commit its policies, resources, and troops to the creation of a viable Kurdish autonomy, let alone an independent state, in part because of Turkish and inter-Arab opposition. Turkey, despite its recently established relations with Iraqi Kurds, is still strongly opposed to an independent Kurdish entity along its border with Iraq, lest this should encourage Kurdish separatism in Turkey or help the PKK guerrillas, or both. For similar reasons, Iran also objects to the creation of a Kurdish entity along its border with Iraq. Saddam's Iraq obviously continues to be vehemently opposed to Kurdish separatism, and it will invest great efforts and various means to this end, including making further concessions to its Shi'i population and playing the Shi'is off against the Kurds. The prospects for the emergence of an all-Iraqi democratic federalist system that would accommodate the divergent interests of the Kurds, Shi'is and Sunnis seem to be very slim, and it is highly probable that any nondemocratic post-Saddam government—whether dominated by Sunnis or by Shi'is—will carry on a similar repressive policy toward the Kurds.

Notes

1. Details in Albert H. Hourani, *Minorities in the Arab World* (London: Oxford University Press, 1947), pp. 91–94; Stephen Hemsley Longrigg, *Iraq 1900 to 1950* (London: Oxford University Press, 1954), pp. 6–12.

2. For a comprehensive study see Nissim Qazzaz, *The Jews in Iraq in the Twentieth Century* (Jerusalem: Yad Yitzhak ben Zvi/Hebrew University Press, 1991; in Hebrew), chapters 2, 3, 5.

3. See Phebe Marr, *The Modern History of Iraq* (Boulder, Colo.: Westview, 1985), pp. 55–76.

4. Qazzaz, *The Jews in Iraq*, pp. 238–245.

5. Arnold Joseph Toynbee, ed., *Survey of International Affairs, 1934* (London: Chatham House, 1935), p. 143. See also R. S. Stafford "Iraq and the Problem of the Assyrians," *International Affairs* 13 (1934), pp. 159–185; John Joseph, *The Nestorians and their Muslim Neighbors* (Princeton, N.J.: Princeton University Press, 1961), pp. 195–213.

6. For an excellent study see Yitzhak Nakash, *The Shi'is of Iraq* (Princeton, N.J.: Princeton University Press, 1994). This section is partly derived from Nakash's study.

7. See Nakash, *The Shi'is*, pp. 113–120,

8. Nakash, *The Shi'is*, pp. 124–125; see Marr, *Modern History*, pp. 62–65.

9. On Qasim and his communist leanings, see Uriel Dann, *Iraq under Qassem: A Political History* (New York: Praeger, 1969), pp. 93–107.

10. See Hanna Batatu, "Iraq's Underground Shi'a Movements: Characteristics, Causes and Prospects," *Middle East Journal*, (1981), pp. 578–594. See also Laurie Mylroie, *The Future of Iraq* (Washington: The Washington Institute for Near East Policy, 1991), p. 19.

11. See Nakash, *The Shi'is*, pp. 137–138; Batatu, "Iraq's Underground," pp. 593–594.

12. See Dann, *Iraq*, p. 43; Marr, *Modern History*, p. 166; Majid Khadduri, *Republican Iraq: A Study in Iraqi Politics* (London: Oxford University Press, 1969), p. 18; Amatzia Baram, *Culture, History and Ideology in the Formation of Ba'thist Iraq, 1968–1989* (New York: St. Martin's, 1991), pp. 7–8.

13. See Baram, *Culture*, pp. 11, 15, see Ronen Zeidel, *The Iraqi Ba'th Party 1948–1995* (unpublished M.A. thesis, Haifa University, 1997; in Hebrew), pp. 33–56.

14. Baram, *Culture*, pp. 15, 19; but see Marr, *Modern History*, p. 282; Zeidel, *The Iraqi Ba'th Party*, pp. 159–170.

15. Zeidel, *The Iraqi Ba'th Party*, pp. 287–295.

16. Baram, *Culture*, pp. 61–68.

17. On the Kurdish national movement in its various phases see Abdul Rahman Ghassemlou, *Kurdistan and the Kurds* (London: Collet's, 1965); Hasan Arfa, *The Kurds* (London: Oxford University Press, 1966); Derk Kinnane, *The Kurds and Kurdistan* (London: Oxford University Press, 1964); Edmund Ghareeb, *The Kurdish Question in Iraq* (Syracuse, N.Y.: Syracuse University Press, 1981); Marion Farouk-Sluglett and Peter Sluglett, *Iraq Since 1958* (London: KPI, 1987); David McDowall, *A Modern History of the Kurds* (London: I. B. Tauris, 1996); Sa'ad Jawad, *Iraq and the Kurdish Question: 1958–1970* (London: Ithaca, 1981); Mahmud al-Durra, *al-Qadiyya al-Kurdiyya* [*The Kurdish Problem*] (Beirut: Dar al-Talia, 1963; in Arabic); Jalal al-Talabani, *Kurdistan wa-l-Haraka al-Qawmiyya al-Kurdiyya* [*Kurdistan and the Kurdish National Movement*] (Beirut: Dar al-Talia, 1971; in Arabic); Ofra Bengio, *Mered Ha-Kurdim Be-Iraq* [*The Kurdish Rebellion in Iraq*] (Tel Aviv: Ha-Kibutz Ha-Meuhad, 1989; in Hebrew).

18. See al-Durra, *al-Qadiyya*, pp. 70–71; see Kinnane, *The Kurds*, pp. 86–87.

19. See W. Eagleton, *The Kurdish Republic of 1946* (London: Oxford University Press, 1963), pp. 53–58. On the Barzani rebellions, see Khalid Salih, *State-Making, Nation-Building and the Military: Iraq 1941–1958* (Göteborg, Sweden: Göteborg University, 1996), pp. 78–82.

20. Salih, *State-Making*, pp. 56–58; Arfa, *The Kurds*, pp. 79–81.

21. Jawad, *Iraq*, p. 38; Ghassemlou, *Kurdistan*, p. 225, Dann, *Iraq*, p. 36.

22. See David Kimche, *The Last Option: After Nasser, Arafat, and Saddam*

Husayn, the Quest for Peace in the Middle East (Tel Aviv: Hotza'at Adanim, 1992; in Hebrew), pp. 199–203. See also Jawad, *Iraq,* pp. 700–706; Michael M. Gunter, *The Kurds of Iraq: Tragedy and Hope* (New York: St. Martin's, 1992), pp. 26–34; and an interview with Mahmud 'Uthman in *al-Wasat,* no. 298, October 13, 1997, pp. 28–30.

23. Details in Ghareeb, *Kurdish Question,* pp. 50–52; Jawad, *Iraq,* pp. 179–183; Bengio, *Mered,* pp. 25–39; Khadduri, *Republican,* pp. 266–278.

24. For the full text see Khadduri, *Republican,* pp. 275–276.

25. Marr, *Modern History,* pp. 222–223; Bengio, *Mered,* pp. 49–52.

26. Michael M. Gunter, "Foreign Influences on the Kurdish Insurgency," *Orient* 34 (1993), pp. 106–115.

27. Marr, *Modern History,* p. 255; Bengio, *Mered,* pp. 170–172; Graham E. Fuller, *Iraq in the Next Decade: Will Iraq Survive until 2002?* (Santa Monica, Calif.: Rand, 1993), pp. v, 9.

28. Details in Gunter, "Foreign Influences," pp. 111–113; Bengio, *Mered,* pp. 189–192.

29. Gunter, *The Kurds,* pp. 19–20; see Fuller, *Iraq,* p. 9.

30. Gunter, "Foreign Influences," p. 114; see also *Turkish Daily News,* June 3, 1992; "Kurdish Leader Talabani on Negotiating—One Day—with Baghdad," *Mideast Mirror* 11, no. 29, February 11, 1997.

31. McDowall, *Modern History,* p. 387. See Stephen Kinzer, "'History's Losers' Fight Neighbors and Each Other, Often Assisted by Foes," *New York Times,* September 4, 1996, p. A9. See also Michael M. Gunter, "The KDP–PUK conflict in Northern Iraq," *Middle East Journal* 50 (spring 1996), pp. 225–241.

32. For a good chronology of events, see the *New York Times* reportage from September 3 through 10, 1996.

33. See James Risen, "U.S. Welcomes Kurdish Leader who Betrayed CIA in Iraq," *New York Times,* July 25, 1998, p. A2; "A Chance for the Iraqi Opposition to Make a Fresh Start?" *Mideast Mirror* 11, no. 3, January 6, 1997; see also *Kurdish Observer,* April 22, 1998.

34. See Barton Gellman, "Kurdish Chiefs End Rivalry in Northern Iraq," *International Herald Tribune,* September 19–20, 1998, p. 5; *Ha'aretz,* September 20, 1998.

Chapter 11

Southern Sudan:
Between Integration and Separation

L ike the unresolved Kurdish issue in Northern Iraq, the problem of southern Sudan also seems to be unresolvable for the foreseeable future. It indeed resembles the Kurdish issue in several aspects, but in many ways it is more complex. Like Iraqi Kurdistan, southern Sudan is located on the periphery of the Arab world, in this case bordering on non-Arab African countries whose populations are related to some southern Sudanese tribes or share ethnic African solidarity with them, or both. But unlike the Kurds in Turkey and Iran, neither these African populations nor their governments have been anxious to unite with the underdeveloped southern Sudan, as they wish to avoid compounding their own economic and social difficulties. While trying to maintain their territorial integrity, these East African states have sought a political solution for southern Sudan's problem, which among other things would preserve the African ethnic cultural character of the South and prevent its forced assimilation—namely, Arabization and Islamization—by Sudanese governments based in the North.

Significantly, for various reasons, most East African states—and indeed many southern Sudanese—have advocated for the creation not of an independent state, but rather of an autonomous region within a federal Sudanese state. Although some Sudanese governments have agreed to such a solution, they have not fully implemented their promises or bilateral accords on this issue. As in the Iraqi Kurdish case, successive Sudanese regimes have attempted to Arabize (and Islamize) the South, and to play off the rivalries among its factions. Moreover, they have adopted brutal measures of repression, exploitation, and starvation.[1]

To be sure, the motives behind such coercive policies and the reasons for the mutual antagonism are much deeper than in the Iraqi Kurdish case. The southern Sudanese constitute about 30 percent of the total population (some 33.5 million) and are largely animist (some 90 percent) or Christian. Sudan as a whole, however, has a Muslim majority, mostly Arab (some 40 percent) or Arabized. (This survey will not deal with the non-Arab Muslim minorities in other parts of Sudan.)

The southerners are divided among several ethnic African groups and a great many tribes, and they speak dozens of dialects, but English is their common language. Arabic is the common language in the North, however. Consequently, not only have northerners and southerners been unable to forge a solid ethnic–national community, but successive Sudanese governments—even before the country's independence—have treated the southerners with contempt, animosity, and brutality, regarding them as pagan, primitive, and fragmented. For example, during Ottoman Egyptian rule in Sudan (1820–1881), many youngsters were abducted from the South as slaves and sold by Muslim slave traders, or conscripted into Muhammad Ali's army.[2] The expansion of Egyptian rule in the South was accompanied by forced Islamization as well as by the proselytizing of European Christian missionaries among southern animists.[3] But suppression, exploitation, and the slave trade were increased still further under the radical Islamic Mahdist state in the Sudan (1881–1898) and deepened the southerners' feelings of aversion, fear, and antagonism toward the Muslim North.[4]

Taking into consideration these emotions and certainly their own interests, the British, who occupied Sudan from 1899 to 1955 in a joint British–Egyptian condominium, sought to separate the South from the rest of Sudan and carry out their "southern policy."[5] Its aims were, first, to stop Islamic Arab religious–cultural penetration, economic exploitation, and the slave trade, while permitting Christian missionary activities and the spread of the English language; and second, to develop an ethnic–cultural identity and an administrative infrastructure in the South. Initially, Great Britain had also entertained the idea of joining southern Sudan to British East Africa, particularly Uganda, to protect its regional strategic interests, including the sources of the Nile. But at the Juba Conference in 1947, under Sudanese and Egyptian pressures, the British adopted a new policy of unification in anticipation of Sudanese independence.

A number of southern tribal chiefs and intellectuals accepted unification with Khartoum and were represented in the newly established Legislative Assembly in 1948 and in the government administration. But many southerners opposed this, among them a military unit that resorted to a short-lived armed rebellion in Torit in 1955.[6] When independence was declared in 1956, some southern parties demanded autonomy for the South within a federal state system. The new democratic parliamentary regime initially tended to adopt this request but subsequently ignored it.[7] The revolutionary military–authoritarian rule of Gen. Ibrahim Abbud, from 1958 to 1964, went further, attempting to impose full control over the South by employing military force and centralized measures in the political, economic, and educational spheres, including harsh restrictions on the Christian missionaries' activities. In the eyes of many southerners, these measures were designed to "destroy the African Negroid personality and identity in the Sudan and to replace it with an Arabicized and Islamicized south, thus driving a wedge of the Arab world deep into the continent."[8]

In reaction, several illegal political and military organizations emerged in the South and in neighboring East African countries—established by refugees from the South—to fight for southern autonomy, self-determination, or independence. The primary organization, the Sudan African National Union (SANU), was established in the early 1960s in Uganda. But its positions shifted between a focus on the political and military struggle and a desire for a federal solution and full independence. William Deng, a founding leader of SANU, advocated a political settlement within a federal system. But the military wing of SANU, *Anya Nya* (literally, snake poison), waged guerrilla warfare in southern Sudan under the leadership of Joseph Oduho, seeking total independence for what it called Azania, the name of an ancient East African kingdom that included the southern Sudanese territory. After the collapse of General Abbud's military regime and the election of a new civilian democratic government, negotiations for a political settlement were conducted in the 1965 "Round Table Conference" between SANU and the new government in Khartoum. But the negotiations failed owing to the wide gap between the two sides, partly caused by Anya Nya pressure on the SANU delegation.[9] This military organization continued its attacks on government troops and installations while taking advantage of the difficult terrain in the South—tropical forests and swamps—as well as of the safe haven in neighboring African countries.

The de facto autonomous southerners continued to be critically divided among rival leaders, tribes, and factions, including three separate southern governments and a few coopted southern parties in Khartoum. In the late 1960s, however, Joseph Lagu, an Anya Nya commander, managed to unify most southern political and military forces under his leadership,[10] while in Khartoum, Gen. Ja'afar Numayri seized power in the military coup of May 1969.

Realizing the devastating toll of the southern rebellion on Sudan's political stability and economic development, Numayri initiated a conciliatory policy toward the South. At an Addis Ababa conference in 1972, Lagu and the Sudanese government signed an agreement on a *hukm dhati* (regional self-government) for the South, with the encouragement of neighboring African states and of the United States. For the first time ever, this agreement granted to the "Southern Region"—comprising the provinces of Bahr al-Ghazal, Equatoria, and the Upper Nile—autonomous government institutions as well as representation in the central government and parliament. It also provided for an autonomous educational system in the South, the rehabilitation of the southern refugees, and the incorporation of Anya Nya in the Sudanese Army.[11] Lagu subsequently joined the Sudanese Army at the rank of major general and was placed in charge of the southern military command. Sudan's constitution of May 1973 stated in the first clause, "The Democratic Republic of the Sudan is a unitary, democratic, socialist, and sovereign republic and is part of both the Arab and African entities."[12]

For several years this remarkable agreement was carried out at a reasonable pace and in an atmosphere of trust and cooperation. This trust and cooperation began to erode, however, particularly after 1976, owing to three new developments and problems that contradicted the southerners' expectations and revived their suspicions. First, the region faced fresh economic difficulties and acute disputes with the central government regarding development projects and a new oil field in the South. Second, Numayri instituted new policies of reinforcing the Arab and Islamic character of Sudan by initiating a rapprochement with Egypt as well as a "national reconciliation" with his Islamic opposition. Thus, in 1977, Numayri coopted the Muslim Brotherhood into his government and appointed its leader, Hasan al-Turabi, as head of a special committee assigned to revise Sudan's new law in conformity with the *shari'a* (Islamic law). In late 1983, the shari'a was indeed applied to the legal system.[13] Third, and simultaneously, Numayri exploited tribal and personal rivalries in the South to play off its leaders against one another. He also decided to redivide the southern region into the three former subregions.

In early 1983, an open rebellion broke out, instigated by a newly established organization named Anya Nya No. 2, attacking government, military, and civilian targets in the South. Amidst further fighting and bloodshed, a new rebel organization was formed, the Sudanese People's Liberation Movement (SPLM). Led by Col. John Garang, a former Sudanese Army officer, this organization, unlike its rival Anya Nya, aimed at toppling Numayri's regime and helping to establish a secular democratic state in the whole of Sudan. Garang's warfare indeed contributed, along with other factors, to the overthrow of Numayri and his regime in April 1985.

The new military government in Khartoum, which lasted

from April 1985 to April 1986, was led by Gen. 'Abd al-Rahman Muhammad Hasan Siwar al-Dahab, and the subsequent elected civilian regime was headed by Sadiq al-Mahdi, leader of the 'Umma party. Both these leaders sought to negotiate with Garang, but neither government was ready to accept Garang's preconditions for negotiations, notably revoking the application of the shari'a in Sudan. Consequently, guerrilla warfare continued and the rebels managed to occupy large parts of the South. The military achievements of the rebels, coupled with severe political and economic difficulties, prompted Prime Minister Mahdi to meet Garang's conditions regarding the shari'a, but Mahdi was overthrown on June 30, 1989 in a military coup led by Gen. Umar al-Bashir, a devout follower of Hasan Turabi. Turabi, head of the National Islamic Front (NIF) subsequently became the speaker of the parliament and perhaps the second most powerful leader in Sudan.

Given its leadership, it is not surprising that the new government in Khartoum has strongly rejected every suggestion to change its Islamic and authoritarian character, as put forward in the renewed negotiations with Garang. Indeed, since 1989, several attempts have been made—mostly by external mediation—to negotiate a new agreement between the government and the rebels: twice in 1989, in Addis Ababa and Nairobi; in Abuja, Nigeria, in 1992; in Kenya and Uganda in 1993; and again in Nairobi in 1994, 1995, 1997, and 1998.[14] All these attempts failed not only because of the Islamic–secular controversy, but also because of the disagreement on the status of the South.

The latter issue has also emerged as a major bone of contention among the rebels, alongside their factional and personal disputes. Garang has continued to adhere to his notion of a "united secular Sudan," including an autonomous federated South; and in 1995 he joined forces with the former prime minister, Sadiq al-Mahdi, leader of the illegal National Democratic Alliance (NDA). On the other hand, a southern splinter group formed in 1991, the Nasir faction, initially struggled for an independent South. In 1996, however, its leaders—like other southern politicians—were coopted by the

Khartoum government.[15]

These internal rivalries among the southerners have also been characterized by periodic armed clashes between various factions and tribes, notably the Dinka and the Nuer. In addition, violent skirmishes have occasionally erupted between Arab and African tribes in the South, and other clashes elsewhere have been instigated by Muslims against Christians.[16] Yet the greatest degree of bloodshed and destruction has been caused by the ongoing but inconclusive war between government troops and some 50,000 rebels. About 1.3 million civilians and soldiers have been killed, not including those victims—mostly children and the elderly—who died from starvation. The war has also led to such atrocities as abductions for slavery, and it has created huge numbers of refugees and displaced persons within Sudan and in neighboring African countries.[17]

Several East African states have periodically provided not only shelter for southern Sudanese refugees, but also safe havens and military assistance to the rebels. Since the 1960s, some of these countries have also occasionally enabled Israel—the only non-African country helping the rebels—to deliver weapons and instructors to the rebels in the South.[18] Among the East African countries, Ethiopia, Eritrea, and Uganda have actively helped the rebels to fight the Khartoum regime in retaliation for its interference in their domestic affairs, particularly for its support of their radical Islamic elements.[19]

Few East African countries have openly supported the secession of southern Sudan, lest this become a precedent for other African states and thus cause instability in the region. They have instead advocated a peaceful political solution to the southern problem within Sudan, also in an attempt to relieve themselves of the burden of the southern refugees. Thus, it is highly unlikely that these countries would participate in a coordinated military effort to split the South from Sudan. There is little support for such an effort on the part of Egypt, the key regional power and Sudan's neighbor, or in Washington, or even among the rebels. For a long period, in fact, Egypt assisted Sudanese regimes, sometimes actively, against the southern separatists. In recent years, however, Cairo has had poor relations with the militant Islamic regime in Khartoum.

As for the United States, in recent years it has rendered financial and military assistance to Ethiopia, Eritrea, and Uganda, which have backed the southern rebels. In December 1997, Secretary of State Madeleine Albright met the rebel leaders for the first time, in Kampala. She reportedly expressed moral support for their struggle against the Khartoum regime and for their own cause—namely, to lay the foundation of a new Sudan in which inhabitants of all religions and cultures will work to rehabilitate their country.[20]

Washington may indeed use the Sudanese opposition, including the southern rebels, to facilitate the overthrow of the militant Islamic regime in Khartoum, given that the regime has a record of supporting international terrorists such as Usama Bin Ladin. The 1998 attacks on the U.S. embassies in Nairobi and Dar es-Salaam, and the subsequent U.S. missile attack on a pharmaceutical plant in Khartoum, certainly reflect U.S.–Sudanese relations. Yet, Washington's possible willingness to provide support for toppling the Bashir–Turabi government does not necessarily imply that Washington would actively help to create an independent southern Sudanese state. As in the Iraqi–Kurdish case, as long as the southern rebels themselves are hopelessly fractured along tribal lines and have been unable to unite long enough to push the government troops out, the United States will hesitate to become involved directly, and certainly not militarily, in the southern Sudanese quagmire. Washington is also not inclined to antagonize its regional Arab allies—notably Egypt—by supporting the division of Sudan. In sum, while the United States seeks to destabilize and cause the collapse of the Khartoum government, it has no vital interest in the creation of a southern Sudanese state.

Notes

1. Foreign Commonwealth Office (FCO), *Background Brief—Sudan* (London: FCO, March 1996), p. 3; Reuters, "Thousands Flee Homes in Sudan As Fighting With Rebels Flares," *New York Times*, January 29, 1997, p. A8; James C. McKinley Jr., "Fueled by Drought and War, Star-

vation Returns to Sudan," *New York Times,* July 24, 1998, p. A1. See also reportage in *Financial Times,* July 2, 1998; and *Ha'aretz,* May 8, 1997, and August 21, 1998.

2. Richard Gray, *A History of Southern Sudan (1839–1899)* (London: Oxford University Press, 1961), pp. 2–8. For other studies on Sudan and its southern region during the nineteenth and twentieth centuries, see Peter Malcolm Holt, *A Modern History of the Sudan, from the Funj Sultanate to the Present Day* (London: Weidenfeld and Nicolson, 1961); idem, *The Mahdist State in the Sudan, 1881–1898: A Study of its Origins, Development, and Overthrow* (Oxford: Clarendon Press, 1970); Mandour El-Mahdi, *A Short History of the Sudan* (London: Oxford University Press, 1965); Mohamed Omer Beshir, *The Southern Sudan: Background to Conflict* (New York: Praeger, 1968).

3. Gray, *History,* pp. 20–27.

4. See Robert O. Collins, *The Southern Sudan: 1883–1892* (New Haven, Conn.: Yale University Press, 1964) pp. 22–83; Gray, *History,* pp. 157–160.

5. See Makki Abbas, *The Sudan Question* (London: Faber and Faber, 1981), pp. 19–20, 173–174.

6. Details in Mahdi, *Short History,* pp. 149–150; Rachel Simon, "The Relations Between the Sudanese Government and the South," *Hamizrah Hehadash,* nos. 3–4 (1978), pp. 231–232.

7. Keith Kyle, "The Southern Problem in the Sudan," *World Today* 22 (1966), p. 514; Joseph Oduho and William Deng, *The Problem of Southern Sudan* (London: Oxford University Press, 1965), pp. 33–35.

8. Oduho and Deng, *Problem,* pp. 38–42. See also Arye Oded "The Southern Sudan Civil War," in Willem A. Veenhoven, ed., *Case Studies on Human Rights and Fundamental Freedoms* vol. 4 (The Hague: Nijhoff, 1976), pp. 237–240.

9. See Kyle, "Southern Problem," pp. 516–518.

10. Simon, "Relations," pp. 242–243.

11. The full text of the agreement can be found in *African Affairs,* 76, no. 303 (April, 1977). See also Saad Eddin Ibrahim, *Ta'mmalat fi mas'alat al-aqaliyyat* [*Reflections on the Minorities Question*] (Cairo: Ibn Khaldun Center, 1992), p. 165.

12. Quoted in Haim Shaked and Yehudit Ronen, "The Ethnic Factor in Sudanese Politics," in Milton J. Esman and Itamar Rabinovich, eds.,

Ethnicity, Pluralism, and the State in the Middle East (Ithaca, N.Y.: Cornell, 1988), pp. 255–256.

13. Ibid., p. 260. See also Yehudit Ronen, *Sudan be-milhemet ezrahim* [*Sudan in a Civil War*] (Tel Aviv: Hakibutz Ha-Meuad, 1995; in Hebrew), pp. 63–66.

14. FCO, *Background Brief—Sudan*, p. 3; Peter Mozyuski, "War Without End?" *New African* (July/August 1998), pp. 16–17. See also the journal *al-Siyasa al-Duwaliyya*, no. 111 (1993), pp. 92–96.

15. Mozyuski, "War Without End?"; *al-Wasat*, no. 144 (1994), p. 26; *al-Wasat*, no. 124 (1994), pp. 21–23; *al-Wasat*, no. 264 (1997), pp. 21–25; see also "Time for a Lebanon-style 'Sudanese Taef,'" *Mideast Mirror* 11, no. 22, January 31, 1997.

16. See "Sudan: The Jebelein Massacre," *Civil Society* no. 54 (Cairo, 1996), pp. 10–11.

17. FCO, *Background Brief—Sudan*, p. 3; "Thousands Flee Homes," *New York Times*; McKinley, "Fueled by Drought and War," *New York Times*.

18. See Mitchell G. Bard, "The Evolution of Israel's African Policy," *Middle East Review* (winter 1998/99), p. 25; Shaked and Ronen, "The Ethnic Factor," p. 258. See also *Ha'aretz*, July 1, 1997, and the interview of Ariel Sharon in *Yediot Ahronot*, May 30, 1997.

19. "'Sudanese Taef,'" *Mideast Mirror*; James C. McKinley Jr., "Sudan's Calamity: Only the Starving Favor Peace," *New York Times*, July 25, 1998, p. A3.

20. *Mideast Report*, January 6, 1997; McKinley, "Sudan's Calamity"; *Ha'aretz*, December 11, 1997.

Chapter 12

Conclusion

U nlike the large ethnic minorities in Southern Sudan and in Northern Iraq, many ethnic and religious groups in the region have in the last several decades undergone a process of integration, accommodation, or adjustment within their states. Small ethnic minorities—such as Circassians in Jordan and Syria, Turkomans in Iraq and Syria, and Armenians in Lebanon and Syria—have been incorporated, to various degrees, into their respective countries' politics and society. Others periodically suffered persecution or discrimination and either emigrated or adjusted to their conditions. One group that has experienced both conditions is the fairly large Kurdish ethnic minority in Syria, which constitutes some 7 percent of the population: Whereas the urban Kurds have almost assimilated, the more numerous Kurdish tribal groups in northern and northeastern Syria have been intermittently subjected to forced Arabization and political discrimination. But, being an isolated ethnic group, the Kurdish tribes have little chance of improving their lot vis-à-vis the powerful Arab nationalist and authoritarian regime in Damascus.

Arab Religious Minorities: Christians, Shi'is, and 'Alawis

As for the non-Sunni Arab communities in the region, they have experienced unequal changes, sometimes even upheavals, in their political status vis-à-vis, and in their relations with, the majority populations or the ruling elites. Christian Arabs have been partly integrated as equals in the political, cultural, and economic life of their respective countries; some have even been intellectual and political leaders. This integration process has been more characteristic of Christians of the upper and middle classes, and of small Christian communities,

101

and it occurred mostly in secular-oriented societies such as Jordan, Syria, Iraq, the Palestinian community, and, periodically, in Egypt. In countries with militant Islamic policies or movements, on the other hand, Christians have been treated with suspicion, hatred, and occasional violence. This has at times been the case in Egypt, in Sudan, and among Palestinians, causing fear and trends of seclusion and emigration among Christians.

A prime example of such treatment is that experienced by the ancient, pre-Islamic, Arabized Coptic community in Egypt. Under liberal, secular-oriented regimes, the Copts actively participated in the Egyptian national movement, in government and public institutions, and in economic enterprises. But, with the growth of radical Islamic and pan-Arab tendencies in Egypt in recent decades, the Copts have suffered from certain political and religious restrictions and from occasional deadly attacks by fanatic Muslims. The Egyptian government has certainly endeavored to protect the Copts from militant Islamic groups and to safeguard their political and legal rights. But the predicament of the Copts—and of some Christians elsewhere—will not change dramatically unless their national communities become more secular, democratic, and liberal.

Another case unique in the region is that of the Christian Maronite community (initially the largest sect) and of other Christian Arab sects in Lebanon. For several decades the Maronites have played a dominant role in cooperation with the Sunni upper class in a pluralist, quasi-democratic, secular Lebanese regime. But the shift in the demographic balance in favor of the Muslim communities, the increased Arab nationalist radicalization, the military Palestinian presence, and the Syrian and Israeli interventions all relegated the Maronites to a defensive, militant, position. Following the bloody and largely communal–religious civil war of 1975–1990, the Christian and Muslim communities received an equal share of power in government institutions, under Syrian dictation. This new equilibrium will likely persist for some time, provided Syrian hegemony continues, Maronite–Sunni cooperation endures, and the Shi'i community is granted an appropriate share in the state's political institutions and financial resources. Otherwise, the Shi'is—as the single largest community in Lebanon, constituting around 30 percent of the population—will further strive to rectify their age-old political inferiority and socioeconomic backwardness. The militant elements among them, such as Hizballah, may even fight for more Islamic influence in Lebanon, thus disrupting the new, fragile, intercommunal coexistence, as well as the continued Syrian presence.

Similarly, the larger Shi'i community in Iraq, at about 60 percent of the population, has for generations been deprived of an equitable share in the Sunni Arab–dominated state institutions and economic resources. On various occasions, notably in the late 1970s and in 1991, militant Shi'is rebelled against the government, their final aim being to create an Islamic–Shi'i Iraq. The brutal crushing of these uprisings, alongside patriotic nationalist motives, have influenced many Iraqi Shi'is to prefer options for full integration and participation in the political and socioeconomic systems, compatible with their demographic strength. It is very likely that Iraqi president Saddam Husayn, while maintaining his strict control and persecuting Shi'i opposition, will indeed incorporate more Shi'is in these state systems, although not in the senior army officers' corps. Furthermore, while trying to forge a common anti-Kurdish stance, Saddam (and probably also his Sunni successors) would work further toward consolidating a Sunni–Shi'i Arab Iraq with a unifying, mild Islamic disposition.

Such a national strategy has already been pursued by Hafiz al-Asad, the 'Alawi president of Syria. The 'Alawi minority regime, in power since 1966, has been confronted with an agitated, sometimes rebellious, Sunni majority population. Less advantageously placed than in the Iraqi case, the 'Alawi minority in Syria is demographically smaller—it comprises only some 12 percent of the populace—as well as religiously heterodox and socially backward. Thus, its domination was for years illegitimate in the eyes of many members of the Sunni Arab majority—some 65 percent of the population—which, unlike the Sunnis in Iraq, had long held power prior to the 'Alawi ascendancy. Despite severe constraints, the Sunni uprisings, and government repression—notably at Hama in 1982—Asad has endeavored to advance the development of a Syrian Arab national community on the basis of Arab national education and indoctrination; an ecumenical, moderate Islamic *ethos;* the integration of other non-Sunni sects; and the coopting of most socioeconomic sectors. At the core of this community, Asad has forged a political and economic cooperation, or alliance, between the 'Alawis and new Sunni elites and middle classes. This alliance will prove essential for the evolution of the new Syrian Arab nation state.

In sum, the powerful authoritarian minority regimes in Syria and Iraq are likely to persist and incorporate more sections of the populations in their respective national communities—provided they sustain and extend the coopting of, or alliance with, influential sectors of the majority populations, and continue to stress the notions of national–cultural Arabism; local patriotism; and broad, sober Islamism. Most religious minorities and small ethnic groups in other Arab countries will probably continue to integrate into, or adjust to, their respective nation states at different degrees and pace. The more secular, liberal, and/or democratic these states become, the more the pace and degree of integration would be advanced.

Ethnic Minorities: Kurds and Southern Sudanese

In contrast to the Arab religious minorities in the region, the large populations of ethnic minorities in southern Sudan and Iraqi Kurdistan are doomed to carry on their struggle for self-determination or self-government until a truly democratic system replaces their authoritarian, repressive governments, or until a powerful international intervention occurs on their behalf. Both options, however, appear remote.

In both cases, a similar and mutually accepted political solution was agreed upon in the early 1970s, namely *hukm dhati*—autonomy or self-government within a federal system. But neither agreement held for long, collapsing instead amid renewed warfare, for the following primary reasons:

- The authoritarian military nature of both regimes and their militant nationalist or radical Islamic policies are, in the long run, incompatible with the minorities' expectations.
- Inherent mutual mistrust and suspicion means the minorities are apprehensive regarding the governments' attempts at centralization, economic control, Arabization, and, in the case of Sudan, Islamization, while the governments are concerned lest self-rule lead to separation and the independence of the minorities' regions.
- The chronic internal strife among these ethnic minorities could be—and indeed has been—exploited by the central governments to undermine the minorities' achievements in the area of self-rule.

It may be assumed that these factors, which brought about the collapse of both agreements on self-government, are not going to change radically in the next several years. Should either of the current regimes in Baghdad or Khartoum be overthrown—particularly if the minority helps in the coup—there is no guarantee that the successor government would grant that group self-rule. Only truly democratic, liberal regimes in Khartoum and Baghdad could perhaps come to terms with their regional minority problem, but the prospect for the emergence of such regimes seems negligible.

Equally slim are the chances for creating independent entities or states in the region of southern Sudan or of Iraqi Kurdistan. For one thing, these minorities lack ethnic solidarity and cohesion, particularly in southern Sudan. Moreover, the countries that border these regions oppose—either strongly or mildly—the creation of new independent entities. For example, East African countries would be reluctant to help dismember Sudan, lest they be dragged into new military conflicts; Turkey and Iran will continue to oppose the creation of a Kurdish state in northern Iraq, lest this encourage their own Kurdish minorities to fight for national self-determination.

Israel for many years had an interest in destabilizing or dismembering Iraq and Sudan—its sworn enemies—and it periodically helped the Kurdish and Southern Sudanese rebels to fight their respective Arab governments. Still, without the cooperation of Iran, Turkey, and the East African countries, Israel was unable to extend meaningful assistance to either of these minorities. Furthermore, following the peace agreements with Egypt in 1979, with the Palestinians in 1993, and with Jordan in 1994, Israel has dropped its military assistance to non-Arab and non-Muslim regional minorities in favor of a long-term reconciliation with the Sunni Arab world.

Israel and the Future of Middle Eastern Minorities

On the face of it, Israeli–Arab peaceful coexistence is not likely to affect the state of the various ethnic and religious minorities in the region, at least in the short run. But in the long run, if Israel's democratic and liberal norms spread among its Arab neighbors, they may perhaps affect (alongside other factors) the positions of certain communities and minority-ruled regimes. For example, peace with Israel may perhaps induce the 'Alawi minority rule in Syria to liberalize its political system, or it may stimulate the Sunni majority community to press for a larger share in power. It may also induce the Shi'ites and other religious groups in Lebanon to struggle together for emancipation from Syrian control.

But these scenarios now seem distant, as Israel has not yet completed its peace process with all of its Arab neighbors. In this context it can be said that Israel's urge to coexist peacefully with its Arab neighbors while preserving its Jewish democratic character is also related to its own policy toward its Arab Palestinian minority and toward the Palestinian Arabs in the West Bank and Gaza. Despite its initial false start and ongoing problems, the process of integrating the Arab Palestinian minority in Israel has been sound. Further improving this process and preventing a possible serious crisis with its ethnic-national Arab minority are additional rationales behind Israel's efforts to seek a negotiated settlement with the Palestine Liberation Organization. Without an agreed solution, Palestinian–Israeli violence may erupt that could perhaps involve Palestinian Arab citizens of Israel and thus reverse the process of their integration. In that case, the implication of Israeli Arabs in terrorist bombings inside Israel in August 1999 may be only the sign of things to come.

Washington and the Middle Eastern Minorities

Even if Israel advances its peace process with the Palestinians and with Syria and Lebanon, the major ethnic conflicts in northern Iraq and southern Sudan will remain unresolved, dangerous, and bleeding. The Iraqi Kurds and the southern Sudanese are likely to receive more U.S. backing to help them forge their de facto self-rule, while Washington will use the two minority groups to topple the regimes in Baghdad and Khartoum. But these minorities cannot expect direct American involvement to help them create independent states in their respective regions. This is because the United States is disinclined either to commit its troops to fight in the Kurdish mountains and Sudan's jungles, or to antagonize its Turkish and Arab regional allies, who oppose Kurdish and South Sudanese independence. By the same token, the United States is not likely to intervene on behalf of other oppressed ethnic minorities and religious communities, such as the Copts in Egypt, the Kurds in Syria, and even the Shi'is in Iraq. It will instead try to avoid alienating its Arab allies and other Arab states while advancing its strategic aims in the Middle East—namely, preventing regional conflicts, resolving the Arab–Israeli dispute, and establishing a regional security system under its auspices.

Nevertheless, the United States can afford to transcend these strategic goals and make more efforts toward settling, or easing, the minorities' problems in several Middle Eastern countries. Thus, Washington should further encourage the formation and development of genuine intercommunal coalitions that strive to replace their oppressive regimes and establish federal democratic systems in their respective countries. The cases in point are a Kurdish–Arab (Shi'i and Sunni) Iraqi group and a Southern–Northern Sudanese coalition. Simultaneously, the United States should induce other countries to uphold the political, cultural, and civil rights of their minorities by including minority rights as a central factor in determining U.S. economic and military assistance. This is particularly relevant to Syria and, to some degree, also to Egypt. Finally, in addition to improving the status of its Kurdish minority, Damascus—which seeks U.S. economic assistance— should be induced to let the Lebanese people sustain independently their pluralist democratic system.

Populations and Minorities
in the Middle East

C hart 1, Overall Regional Figures, looks at the core region—Egypt, Sudan, Iraq, Syria, Lebanon, Jordan, the
Palestinian Authority, and Israel—in round numbers. Chart
2, Division by Countries, shows most recent population figures available for each country.

Sources for both charts: CIA, *The World Factbook 1998*
(online: http://www.odci.gov/cia/publications/factbook/
sy); Saad Eddin Ibrahim, *An English Abstract of Sects, Ethnicity
and Minority Groups in the Arab World* (Cairo: Ibn Khaldun
Center for Development Studies, 1994), pp. 8, 19; R. D.
McLaurin, ed., *The Political Role of Minority Groups in the Middle
East* (New York: Praeger, 1979), pp. 268–287.

Chart 1: Overall Regional Figures			
Religion	**Arab/Arabized**	**Non-Arab**	**Total**
Sunni Muslim	98 million	18 million	116 million
Shi'i and Heterodox Muslim	18 million	—	18 million
Animist	—	10 million	10 million
Jewish	—	5 million	5 million
Christian	4 million	8 million	8 million
Total	120 million	37 million	157 million

Chart 2: Division by Countries

Country	Population	Religious Communities		Ethnic Groups	
Egypt	66,050,004	Sunni Muslim:	94%	Arab, Berber, and Arabized Hamite:	99%
		Copt, other Christian: (official estimate)	6%	Greek, Nubian, Armenian, other:	1%
Iraq	21,722,287	Shi'i Muslim:	60–65%	Arab:	75%–80%
		Sunni Muslim:	32–37%	Kurdish:	15%–20%
		Christian and other:	5%	Assyrian, other:	5%
Israel	5,643,966 (c. 6 million in 1999)	Jewish:	82%	Jewish:	82%
		Sunni Muslim:	14%	Non-Jew (mostly Arab):	18%
		Christian:	2%		
		Druze and other:	2%		
Jordan	4,434,978	Sunni Muslim:	96%	Arab:	98%
		Christian:	4%	Circassian:	1%
				Armenian:	1%
Lebanon	3,505, 794	Shi'i Muslim:	25%–32%	Arab:	95%
		Sunni Muslim:	20%	Armenian:	4%
		Maronite Christian:	20%	Other:	1%
		Druze:	7%		

		Religion		Ethnicity	
		Armenian:	6.5%		
		Greek Orthodox:	11%		
		Greek Catholic:	7.5%		
		Other Christian:	3%		
Palestinian Authority (West Bank and Gaza)	c. 2,500,000	Sunni Muslim:	96%	Arabs	100%
		Christian:	4%		
Sudan	33,550,552	Sunni Muslim:	70%	Black African:	52%
		Animist:	25%	Arab:	39%
		Christian:	5%	Beja:	6%
				Foreign:	2%
				Other:	1%
Syria	16,673,282	Sunni Muslim:	74%	Arab:	85%
		'Alawi:	11.6%	Kurdish:	7%
		Druze:	3%	Armenian:	4%
		Greek Orthodox:	4%	Other:	4%
		Armenian:	4%		
		Syrian Catholic:	1.2%		
		Greek Catholic:	1.2%		
		Shi'i, Syrian Christian, Isma'ili, Protestant:	1%		